ALWAYS FAITHFUL, ALWAYS FREE

by

Thurman I. Miller

Edited by David T. Miller

Always Faithful, Always Free

iUniverse books may be ordered through booksellers or by contacting:

iUniverse
1663 Liberty Drive
Bloomington, IN 47403
www.iuniverse.com
1-800-Authors (1-800-288-4677)

ISBN: 978-0-595-52660-4 (pbk)
ISBN:978-0-595-62714-1 (ebk)

Printed in the United States of America

As always, this book is dedicated to my beloved Recie

- Thurman Miller

Editor's Note

Ten years ago my understanding of my father's life was fragmented. I knew he had been a Gunny Sergeant in the U.S. Marine Corps, serving in the South Pacific on Guadalcanal and elsewhere in the Solomon Island chain. I knew that experience had shaped his character in ways that would resound through my life, and my children's lives. I knew he had grown up very poor in a huge family in a remote "holler" near Mullens, West Virginia, and had heard him talk about the Roaring Twenties, the Great Depression, FDR, riding in a car for the first time, hearing his first radio. I knew he had spent decades as a coal miner, working in some of the harshest conditions a human can endure.

But there were many gaps in my understanding, and it was sometimes hard to reconcile the different parts of his story. He was a trained killer in World War II, ruthless and tough; but he was also the guy who always had a joke ready, always stopped to help a neighborhood kid with some project. His experience in the South Pacific jungle left him with recurrent bouts of malaria that severely restricted what he could eat, and an incurable fungal infection ate away at his fingernails and toenails. Yet he never complained. He had only a high school education, but read widely—history, science, current events, how-to books.

And he wrote. After the war, my father bought a portable Royal typewriter and wrote as a form of therapy for what we would now call post-traumatic stress disorder. He never intended for anyone else to read it; the act of putting his thoughts and memories down was enough, as if in doing so he could rob them of their sting. By the time he agreed to let me read what he had written, he had a huge stack of material—his account of the war and the mines, but also short stories, historical sketches of his grandfather and other "old-timers," mountain and farming lore, and on and on. I was astonished at the amount and breadth of what he'd written, and reading it gave me the gift of a rounded understanding of the special person he is. A good man, living as fully as possible the life he's been given, his gratitude for the small happiness of everyday life made visible against the dark background of war's death and sacrifice.

I've edited numerous books and began to suggest to my father that he publish his writing as a memoir. He refused for years, with typical modesty. Too much of his writing is personal (and not always flattering to its author), so it's understandable he would be reluctant to let just anyone read it. But with the passing of so many of his friends, and the arrival of what he calls his "dividend years"—those following the Bible's proverbial three score and ten—he finally agreed. We began work on the first of three planned volumes, and *War and Work: The Autobiography of Thurman Miller* was published in 2001. The book was an immediate, if modest, hit, leading to newspaper articles about him, book signings, television appearances, and the thrill of seeing his own name along the spine of a book in Beckley's Tamarack and many other bookstores. He heard from long-lost service buddies and was asked to speak at various veterans' events. Because of its original material about World War II, libraries from New Zealand to Norway ordered copies of the book. I was gratified that this member of the Greatest Generation had lived long enough to be recognized for an extraordinary life, spanning horse and buggy days through the moon landing, the Internet, gene therapy, and so much more. As he says, it's been an amazing time to have been alive.

For the second book, *Coal Bloom*, I was fortunate to track down many of the men he'd served with in K Company, First Marine Division. We recorded many conversations and asked the men to follow up with their own written recollections of their time in the South Pacific, and those materials supplemented his own memories to paint a vivid picture of life on the front lines on the Island of Death, Guadalcanal. *Coal Bloom* also pulled together a great deal of mountain and farming lore from his childhood in the twenties and thirties, lore that very few today know, even the old-timers. The book was also successful, filling a unique place in the written history of West Virginia and its sons. It also triggered a visit from the National World War II Museum in New Orleans, which conducted a long interview with my father as background material for Museum displays. He also provided primary source material for an upcoming television miniseries initiated by historian Stephen Ambrose about the men of K Company, a companion piece to HBO's historic Band of Brothers series.

As I write this, my father approaches his eighty-ninth birthday. His steps are slower, but he still has the same can-do spirit, still works in his wood shop a few hours every day, still strives to learn something new every day. He mastered e-mail years ago and keeps in touch with friends all over the world, and surfs the Internet for whatever subjects interest at the time. His humor and curiosity are still strong, even as his body begins to fail him.

The book you now hold, the third and final volume of his life story, is a benediction and summing-up. The war still throws its long shadow down the years, and still more near-forgotten mountain customs are documented, but the entire book is a love letter of sorts to his West Virginia homeland, to the brave comrades of the First Marine Division left behind in the South Pacific, and to the woman with whom he shared this extraordinary life. Early this year we buried my mother, his soul mate and partner of sixty-two years, and his tender care for her in her long decline was the greatest monument he could have built to the gentle woman he'd courted as a teenager. None of us could wish for more in our lives than that sort of devotion.

My father's life is a testament to some very basic principles, as hard-won as that knowledge can be. Make do with what you have, where you are. Love your country. Help someone less fortunate than you. Express your gratitude every day. Enjoy the little things. Stay curious. Laugh.

And: No greater love has any man than this, that he would lay down his life for his friend.

So, we hope you enjoy *Always Faithful, Always Free* as much as we have enjoyed putting it together. This and the two previous volumes demonstrate some of the strength and resilience of mountain people, and we hope these books encourage you to share your stories with your children, and to seek out those of your elders. In the end, all we have is each other, and our stories.

David Miller
Editor

A Note on the Title

Our title refers to the two main pillars of my father's life, his love for his home state of West Virginia and his pride at having being able to honorably serve his country in combat in the U.S. Marine Corps. Marines greet each other with *Semper Fi*, or always faithful, and the state motto of West Virginia is *Montani semper liberi*, Mountaineers are always free.

The title is also a tribute to Recie Marshall Miller, beloved wife and mother. When love is faithful, we are free to love completely, without reservation or boundary. Love of that kind is too rare in this world, and we celebrate it.

Editor

Foreword

From the other side of the world, my path has crossed with living history--a man who, ten years before I was born, put his life on the line for me and all Australians. It was World War II and America deployed troops in the first land offensive against the Japanese Empire on a small, wretched island in the South West Pacific named Guadalcanal. The spirit of the American people had united into a collective force of military efficacy following Pearl Harbor. Australia, very small in terms of men and material, was facing destruction as Japan prepared to invade to cut off U.S. supply lines and prevent a military buildup that would threaten Japan's expansionism.

Australia needed help, and America came to our aid. Australians and Americans fought and died together in the Pacific, creating a "family bond" between our nations.

To me, Thurman Miller embodies the spirit of all those American men on that island, and the American people who sacrificed so much in so many ways to support them. As a result of their altruism, I have enjoyed a free life, with children, grandchildren and many wonderful friends. Thurman has been a blessing, as I have been searching for more than twenty years for a way to say thank you to the American people. I have been graciously given that opportunity by way of this introduction.

Many years ago, I began to question the Hollywood portrayal of the war in the Pacific. I made several trips to Guadalcanal in the Solomon Islands to see for myself the battlefields and rusting relics not yet consumed by the jungle. The heat was incessant, absolutely unbearable. I would sweat continuously all day and developed skin sores and rashes. Despite the luxury of modern medicine I was still greatly concerned about malaria and frequently applied insect sprays that were instantly washed off by sweat. These sprays also irritated my skin and eyes and I began to curse the jungle. I drank the local water and became quite sick, lost weight and almost had to leave for Australia just to recover.

My four wheel drive was unable to get through the grass around Bloody Ridge, where the Americans had dug in during that famous battle. The grass was six to nine feet high and razor sharp. I suffered many cuts to my hands and legs that became infected and required daily treatment. Crossing crocodile-infested rivers around the battlefields I quickly discovered my personal fear boundaries. Reminders of the war were everywhere, and I imagined what had taken place during the war at each location. I tried in vain to imagine the Americans enduring such fetid and dangerous conditions whilst under fire.

In the evening I would return to my hotel and the luxury of a cool shower, hot meal, and floor show by the local dance group. After leaving Guadalcanal I looked back at those luxuries with contempt and shame for such comforts. It was clear that Thurman and his fellow servicemen experienced a very different environment than I had!

I have written many articles on the war in the past twenty years, made many trips to Guadalcanal, and undertaken thousands of hours of research. Still, I am still unable to grasp the reality faced by these heroic men. It is only through the writing of men such as Thurman Miller that we can gain an understanding of the truth and power of the human spirit in such conditions. These men demonstrated the unique ability to face adversity and hardships head on, prepared to pay any price and even forfeit one's own life to secure peace and liberty for their fellow man.

This very proud Australian humbly thanks the American people and in particular my good mate of more than ten years, Thurman I. Miller.

16 Chester Street,
Inverell NSW 2360
Australia

The Southern Cross.

Acknowledgements

In the writing and editing of this and the author's two previous books we have had the support and assistance of friends and family far too numerous to fully list, but a few deserve special mention. The surviving members of the First Marine Division were always generous with their time and encouragement, and they will always be my brothers. Maple Fork Baptist Church provided material and spiritual support to our whole family during some very difficult times, for which we'll always be thankful. Thomas Nguyen Naquin of the National World War II Museum in New Orleans conducted a long interview with the author for the Museum's archives, and we are humbled that he and so many others are taking the time to document our generation's spirit and sacrifice. The author had a long association with the West Virginia chapter of the First Marine Division, and veterans young and old there remind us that Marines have bravely defended their country in every decade of its existence, and do still. Dr. Joanna Roberts and her staff of the Rhodell Health Clinic have been a godsend for our family and for everyone in our coal camp area. Her care has helped the author reach the advanced years that at one time seemed unlikely, given the physical toll taken by war and coal mining.

The Tamarack in Beckley carried my books as soon as they were published, and I appreciate their exposing them to the hundreds of thousands of visitors who pass through there; it's an honor to be among the best of West Virginia's artists and craftspeople. Thomas Stearns of Jorkens Books has also been an enthusiastic supporter, and a great host for book signings. WLEX television in Lexington, Kentucky, aired an extensive interview with the author soon after the tragic events of September 11, 2001, helping to put current world events into the broader context of America's ongoing battle to preserve the freedom we enjoy but do not always appreciate. The author was a founding member of the Winding Gulf Restoration Organization (WGRO) of Helen, WV, a good example of what a small town can accomplish with few resources but a great sense of pride in its heritage. The author's sons and daughter and their spouses have supported and encouraged his writing, and their kindness and patience toward their mother in her last earthly days were worth more than any father could ask. My youngest son, David, the editor of all three of my books, had the vision and energy to turn a large stack of paper with various memories into real books. From tracking down old Marine buddies for interviews to shaping and reshaping the final form of the books to designing the covers, this has clearly been a labor of love, and a great journey to have made together. My Australian friends have been generous as well. Ken James of Snake Valley, Australia (www.astroken.bravehost.com) very kindly supplied beautiful photos of the Southern Cross constellation. Rob Crawford of New South Wales has always been a great supporter of my writing, for which I'm very grateful. Finally, my greatest thanks and love go to

Recie, my wife and partner of sixty-two years, my nurse when I was sick, my light in the darkness, my reason for living in the early days after the war, when I did not think I could. Now she has gone on ahead, and I look forward to reuniting with her.

Thurman Miller

1

Just Thinking

WHEN WE SEE AN ELDER sit with elbow on knee and folded fist under chin we know his mind is at work and his thinking spans the years. He may be sorting out the thoughts he will pass on to his children and grandchildren, as he wishes to leave a portrait of himself and his times. Age, as we call it, is a relative term. Now, at the age of 88, my body reminds me clearly of it. Time passes. I have learned that it remains for each of us to use time as it passes by. Someone may need only a kind word. A boy may need the tires pumped up on his bike, or a car may be stalled on a highway. There are needs everywhere, everyday. If we miss a chance to help those who need it, we have wasted a portion of our time. It has passed on forever. Time passes.

But in my mind, time is elastic. I can be very young, a teen again, a Marine, a miner, father, grandfather. Now that I have written two books, what else is there still to say? I made this same remark several years ago and realized, back then, that many things enter one's mind when he is not even aware of it. Thoughts pass with no speculation on their significance. Many seemingly unimportant thoughts slip way unnoticed, but I think they should be granted a few lines on which we may reflect in days, months and years to come. Little things one's mother or father, who cared so much for us, may have said, or my siblings, whom I described in *Coal Bloom*.

As I celebrate my eighty-eighth birthday I sit and ponder. I think back to my own father at this age. He was this age at his passing. What must he have been thinking as he turned this age? It's something I cannot grasp. I can only remember him as he aged along with my mother, and I cherish those bygone days as we watch them on my old home movies.

One thing I have never discussed with anyone is the last days of my parents or my siblings as they each bid farewell to this vale of tears. I was at the bedside of only my sister Kathleen, and in her last days her mind wandered far and wide and her subconscious led her to say things that she would normally have never said or.

A few nights before Kathy died I had a dream which I have never told to anyone except my wife Recie. I could tell her because down through the years she had witnessed, lying beside me as I slept, the outward effect of many of my dreams. Some were nightmares and some merely mingled my war and my work, both themes of my life coming together in a single dream.

But this particular dream featured my parents, Eli and Elvira. In the small post office in Helen there was, in my dream, a small snack shop with just two booths. I stood alone at the bar. It was raining very hard. The stream that ran in front of the post office was swollen almost out of its banks. From the rear entrance of the post office came my mother and father. Dad was dressed plainly in overalls, as was always his way, while Mother wore a polka-dot dress with dots about the size of eggs. Dad strode a few paces ahead of mother. Neither paid attention to me; their minds were clearly on more pressing matters. They strode past me out into the rain and disappeared.

I wondered about seeing my late parents in this dream. Kathy had some unfinished business on this earth that only she and God knew about. In the few days before she died Kathy began to call out all the names of her brothers and sisters. She would pause and speak to her mother alone. "No, mommy, I can't go yet." Then she would repeat the process. Kathy passed from this life very quietly and I remembered that my mother's prayers always ended the same way: "And Lord, give me a peaceful hour in which to die." I believe in my heart she attended Kathy's departure, and the Lord granted her prayer.

Remembering saying goodbye to Kathy inevitably brought back memories of burying our mother and father as well. On a very snowy evening in February, 1966, he was very ill and agreed to go to the hospital. Not willing to cross Tams Mountain in a snow storm I took him to Wyoming General in Mullens. I sat with him in the evening until ten-thirty, when I would go home to rest before returning to the mines the next day. Three nights after he was admitted to the hospital I got a call at one-thirty in the morning. The nurse informed me of his passing. The next morning I went up to his house, where young David had spent the night with Kathy and Elvira, to break the news to them. I came home and picked up the phone to begin calling my many brothers and sisters. It being a party line, someone was already talking. Half an hour later I tried again, with the same result. Half an hour later, same thing. I cut in on their conversation. "I am sorry to interrupt you, but my father passed away last night and I need to phone my family. As soon as I am finished you can resume." For the next few days anytime I picked up the phone it was available. The good folks on the party line demonstrated the usual courtesy of mountain people.

Then on Mother's Day the next year we buried our mother, Elvira. And what a tribute that this mother of fifteen kids was called home on that particular day!

But with her gone it seemed as if the anchor of the ship of life had been lifted and our family was set adrift. It seemed to become more important that we make an effort to connect, and not just meet up at funerals. I started a family reunion in the early 80's and it has grown to include our Miller and Meadows clans and also the Rineharts, my mother's maiden family. These three families have a long and varied history and have produced a huge number of offspring. The first reunion saw fifty-five relatives gathered, while 2007's numbered one hundred and eighteen.

When I served in the Marines the words "family" and "back home" were the most repeated words during any conversation. It has been, and it continues to be, the highlight of my year to have our family together in this way. Younger faces replace older, but we always remember our elders and keep their memories with us on these special days.

Some people go through their lives never knowing that they have kinfolk living next door to them, and it's a sad commentary when kin fail to connect. Much family history is lost forever by this very form of neglect. Every July when our family reunion time arrives I reserve the shelter again for the next year, over a year in advance, when it will again be a time to be together and remember those who have gone on before.

Watching and listening to our neighbor and longtime friend Ann, whose memory is fading fast, or talking to my sister Gladys and remembering our dear mother, makes me wonder about life's strange quirks and strange turns of event. For example, the question comes to mind, when one reaches the age when memory is fading or indeed gone, where did it go? I know science and the world of medicine have many theories as to what takes place in the human brain. But where did the memories go? Are they with God? Do they lie submerged deep within the recesses of the brain, where they sleep for eternity?

The scriptures teach us, as does everyday experience, that the wind bloweth where it listeth, and we cannot tell where it came from or where it is going except by looking at its effects. We see trees bending in certain directions and know the wind travels that way. But where has it gone? As with the brain and its reservoir of knowledge buried forever, so is the wind gone. We see these effects in a person affected with Alzheimer's disease, just as we see the devastation of tornados, but never the wind itself.

And where does time go? Time is the perpetual motion of humanity. It flows on and on by us each second, each minute, hour, day and year. We cannot control it. We cannot recycle it as I do a piece of wood. We can only use that little portion of it allotted to us. It goes on and on and it is left up to each individual as to what he will do with it. To use an analogy from my electrical training, time is the very essence of what we call direct current. It flows only one way, and once it passes it is gone. We use three days to describe our existence, yesterday, today and tomorrow. Yesterday is gone and we have no promise of tomorrow. Today is our time. Let us use it wisely. We can waste it but we cannot slow its passing.

2

School Days

I WATCH THE NEWS AS it covers graduations, and the young, eager faces give me renewed hope for the coming years. In our society this is a happy period, as families prepare their children, now adults for all practical purposes, for college. Granddaughter Molly, David's eldest, just graduated from high school, reminding me of my own schooling. Pomp and circumstance were more subdued in those Depression and pre-war days. But nevertheless we had both baccalaureate and graduation ceremonies, where we were seated boy, girl, boy, girl. I sat between two very pretty girls and at rehearsal they asked me to bring extra handkerchiefs because they knew they would cry (and indeed they did).

As I described in *Coal Bloom*, I attended a two-room school at Otsego through the sixth grade. There were only two of us in that grade for the whole year. Then, in the middle of the Depression, I started at Mullens High in the seventh grade. But I had left the protective umbrella of Effie A. "Granny" Delp, about whom I wrote at length in my prior books. I missed her personal touch, her one-on-one assistance, and I quit school two months before the year was over. The next year, realizing I had missed something, I went back and told the principal I wanted to start over. During the next six years I came to love the old school. It was always an honor to tell people I went to Mullens High. John D. Farmer was principal and I still laugh at the sound of his high raspy voice yelling, "All right you flappers!" I found out that year that Mullens High teachers also took a personal interest in their children, and although I did not apply myself as I should have I did graduate with the class of '39.

My brother Gilbert in front of a Mullens landmark the Depot Lunch.

One oddity I remember is that during these years there were four different custodians of the school. Their names were Biggs, Little, Long and Short.

One of the most influential teachers I ever knew as Mary Staats. She was the mentor, teacher, friend, and in many cases, a second mother to her kids at Mullens High School and Otsego School. She was there during some of the same years as Granny Delp, and both came to our home for dinner many times. They were both a great help to my family in many ways. Mrs. Staats took my wife Recie into the first grade at Otsego and then twelve years later was her teacher and home room sponsor when Recie graduated from Mullens High in 1943.

I was privileged to have her husband, Bill Staats, as one of my teachers at Mullens High. As did Mary, he took his profession beyond the normal duties of teacher and made his students feel at ease regardless of their social standing, manner of dress or scholastic abilities. They were both totally dedicated to their profession as teachers. The teachers had the children of the Depression but were able, somehow, to deal with the scarcity of food and clothing and school supplies. They also had the children of war, and they sought to not only educate their charges in the three "R's" but also teach them (us) how to deal with the serious challenges we were facing. Mr. and Mrs. Staats were sincere in what they believed and serious in what they taught, and their students left their charge with much information that would sustain them in adulthood.

As I view various old photos I also notice how drastically the dress code has changed down through the years. Old Sunday School photos show all the boys wore bib overalls and for some reason they always left one gallous loose. The girls did not fare any better, for their clothes were mostly homemade from feed sacks. My mother, like many women of her generation, was endowed with a wisdom born of necessity; she could make do with whatever was on hand. Though the clothing back then was simple it was always clean. Today's schoolchildren also have their own style of dress. Some schools have adopted uniforms and sometimes that works, but today's youth seem to like their own styles, and to me that's a good thing. Children all dressed identically promotes a high degree of regimentation and in the long run takes away kids' individualism.

School busses crowd the highways and children with backpacks wait along the road. In my school days there were no such things as backpacks. Most children took their books home tied with an extra belt or a piece of string.

June brings an all-year reunion of my high school. I suppose school consolidation is necessary but something is lost in the process. Mullens High School is no more, a victim of the trend toward larger, consolidated schools. The last Rebel Yell has reverberated through the mountains, and when its echo fades Mullens High will be but a whisper.

As kids return to school each fall I pray that this year no shots will ring out at random, no tears will be shed for a student, or for the young shooters themselves. We realize no one person is to blame for the

Yours truly. I have been told our family has both Cherokee and Melungeon blood.

repetition of these senseless acts, but we can lay much of the blame on "progress." During the Depression, young people weren't exposed to a life of drugs, violence and death. We devised our own type of play, with games like shinny and ante-over. But with the Great War came the separation of families. Fathers, brothers and sons went off to war. Women, with the advent of "Rose the Riveter," went to work. Family life as we knew it broke down, never to be the same. So let us hope this year will be a safe one for the children. Let them attend school in peace and come home to an atmosphere of love, knowing they have someone who cares.

West Virginia's Senator Jay Rockefeller was on the news recently, promoting his efforts to get a prison built in McDowell County. It would, he said, bring many jobs into the county. He deserves praise for that goal, as that county needs a boost from anyone who can produce it. At about the same time a group of journalists from one of the major television networks had been all over the U.S. taking pictures of schools in the worst condition. They showed one in McDowell County on the evening news.

Certainly, the country needs prisons, but it makes me wonder about our priorities. The schoolchildren of our state should have first priority for public funds, for their future is determined at the very beginning of their lives. If they have no good, solid, safe schools, they indeed run the risk of winding up in one of our fancy new prisons.

I see another kind of graduation ceremony on the evening news, on the other side of the world. The Taliban of Afghanistan had held school for more than a hundred of their youth in one village, their schooling gearing them for death and the destruction of our American way of life.

They were schooled in how to build bombs and fit them around their bodies. After they "graduated" they were given their mission. Each was told to move to a country, get established, and await orders to enter a designated place and blow up themselves and as many of us "infidels" as possible. Their young teen faces appeared devoid of emotion. It occurred to me than they had no hope for the future and were willing to end it all to please these agents of death, believing they would inherit a place in heaven. What a glaring difference in the commencement ceremonies of our two countries.

3

Pastimes

COUSIN ANNIE IS THE DAUGHTER of Hiram Rinehart, my uncle, and she has preserved many memories from her childhood, no doubt from listening to her older siblings and parents. As I talk to Annie we discuss the old days, when they lived on the mountaintop above Mullens. We talk about the old grapevines that grew on the mountain, and the swings her brother Johnny made from steel cables. Grapevine swings were a given for whatever hillside we played on, but cousin Johnny worked for the power company and one day brought home a long piece of three-eighths-inch steel cable. He climbed atop a large tree and attached the cable to a stout limb. We'd pull the cable and the seat to the highest point we could and hop on. Down the hill and over the brink we went. If we had fallen it would have been at least a hundred-foot drop, but we took chances in those days. Fortunately, no one was killed or seriously injured on either the cable swing or the natural grapevines.

Growing up in the hills meant walking barefoot in the grass and even into forested areas as soon as the weather warmed a little in the spring. My feet hardened to walking, running and jumping, but many times I got what we called stone bruises. I recall once having four of them at the same time and, believe it or not, I crawled about until they healed. (Stupidly, I had jumped off a tool shed into a pile of rocks.)

When I was growing up on our farm, every summer we would construct a small dam so we could swim. We would pick out a place on Cedar Creek where there was already a long pool with few rocks. These ponds were where we fished in the summer. We cut down enough small trees to build a dam about four feet high, always making sure the trees were longer than the creek was wide. On each side of the stream we dug a short trench and placed the first log in the creek as close to the bottom as possible. Then we began filling the dam with sod. We picked a place with a good growth of grass and cut large chunks of sod and began filling the in behind the first log. Then we put the second log in place and repeated the sodding and logging until the dam was finished. If we noticed a leak, someone grabbed the shovel and headed for the grass to get a chunk of sod.

These small dams provided us a place to cool off and play on many hot evenings. The upper end of the dam pool was left shallow, so little kids could wade. We used the pool throughout the early summer months until the heat dried the creek to a mere tickle. In late summer the pool dropped to about a foot deep. At that point I would pull up a log and let the whole pool out at once. (Once I accidentally released enough water to wash away Uncle

Bill Rinehart's submerged wash tub, where he kept all his bait minnows. He was agitated, to say the least.)

Once when I was just a youngster in my early teens I loved to climb trees to their very tops. You might say I was part monkey. One particular pine tree always fascinated me as I passed by. It was at least sixty feet high and the boughs were plentiful. I studied this tree and one day I decided to conquer it. It was a good climb going up. Plenty of limbs to grasp and pull myself upward. Finally I reached to top and was able to see all around. While watching the birds in the air and an occasional rabbit below I became lost in thought and forgot exactly where I was. Suddenly I lost my balance and began to tumble down. Quickly noticing how the boughs supported me I just let them bear me gently from one bough to the next until the last one deposited me gently on terra firma.

Me as a baby with family friend Jim Vaughn.

These days it seems like every child is issued a cell phone at birth. My own experience with telephones began in seventh grade. I was just starting school when I was summoned to the principal's office with a message that I was wanted on the phone. Well, by golly, that was something! Very timidly I picked up the phone and said, hello. I heard nothing.

Very gently the secretary took the receiver out of my hand and reversed ends with it. She said nothing, I said nothing. Of course I was embarrassed, but I told myself that a person learns something new every day! Can you imagine a seventh-grader today not knowing how to use the phone? But you have to remember there were very few phones in homes at that time. Many did not even have power, much less a phone. After I came home from the Marine Corps and built a home up Cedar Creek, above Mullens (as described in *War and Work)* the phone company ran a line up to our property. Our very first phone was a party line with eight people on it. There were, indeed, no secrets in the hollow. We'd dial the operator and give her the number we wished to call. They were easy to remember—ours was just 70J2. Today, when your phone rings the voice on the other end may be human or only a pre-recorded message. But even if you make the call yourself the voice answering is often synthetic, and it gives you several options to choose from, sometimes far too many. You choose an option and then another voice gives more options and so on and on until finally in total frustration you begin to punch 0 and 0 and 0. Only then do you hear a voice which doesn't sound like a machine.

It's a rare thing for a kid of seven not to know how to operate a computer, not to mention high tech equipment of every kind. I could not in my wildest dreams compete with any of my grandchildren in this area now. They have me beat, but it's fun trying to learn. (I wrote this book on my newest computer, having worn out three already.)

One of the Depression-era events the young ladies of the day took special pride in was the box supper, or pie supper. They would construct their own box supper with whatever they desired to put into it. Some were more elaborate than others, depending on their family's level of affluence. It was usually just some sandwiches, homemade cookies, and a slice of favorite pie, but some went so far as to fry chicken and all the trimmings to go with it.

At Helen Baptist. At one time, truly a gathering place for the whole town.

The box supper was always well attended. Bear in mind that there were no televisions, computers, or DVDs, and few radios back then, and an event such as this was a good place for youth to come together. Young coal miners came with their meager paydays and the boxes were held up for them to bid on, and all the girls sought to make their box as attractive as they could. As the bidding began, whispers circulated throughout the room as to who brought that particular box, and the popularity war was on. The prettier the girl and the prettier the box, the higher the bid. This kind of event raised money for schools and community projects, usually organized by the teacher. Our own beloved Granny Deep was very active in this respect.

The box supper passed on into oblivion with the coming of prosperity after World War Two and the packaging of frozen and precooked food.

I recall many of the games we played at recess. Alas, schools no longer have the pleasure of a simple game like tag, for touch games have come to be regarded as dangerous. At any rate we were outside in fresh air running and playing, and these are cherished memories.

But my encounter with the world of organized sports was brief. In the seventh grade I went out for basketball, and everyone who joined the team got to play. I got to go to Pineville and play in the tournament for my grade. I remember not knowing much about the game but I was very active and tried my best. I played as hard as I could. I don't remember who won but that was not for me to worry about—I was just glad I got to play in a tournament.

In my freshman year I took a notion to play football. I was, and am, not very big. But I could run, and I doubt that any team member could outrun me at that age. I reported for practice along with the rest of the team and practiced as hard as any of them. I really looked forward to playing on the high school team. But when I stayed after school to practice I got home well past supper time. I saw, without anything being said, that Dad looked worn out and I knew he had been gathering the crops for the coming winter. I decided then and there I needed to quit the team and help with the harvest. After all, that was all we had to have to live on during the winter months. Pigskin is not edible. I have never regretted my decision.

Spin the bottle sounds boring, does it not? Well, it wasn't. In fact it was the highlight of any party we were invited to attend. The game was played indoors in the living room of whatever family hosted the party. Usually a girl planned it all. The furniture was moved to the walls and chairs placed around the room in a huge circle, as large as the room permitted. The first player went to the center and looked all around at the girls, hoping that when he spun the bottle it would point at one in particular. Sometimes it did and sometimes it didn't. Whoever it pointed to got to take a walk into the next room with the spinner and do some kissing. (Just kissing, mind you, for in those days there was never anything else going on behind closed doors.) It was fun getting to kiss a few girls, pretty or not, and when there are no lights beauty is not a problem.

4

Remedies

CHILDREN GET SICK. WHEN THEY do it can be a terrible time for parents. Remembering the times when our own children got sick I can think back now and wonder how we kept from accidentally killing them, for in our ignorance we allowed them to do things unheard of now. For example, when Gilbert was about six we saw him and other children playing with paint, and paint in those days contained a great deal of lead. I was painting the banisters around the porch and noticed the boys playing with paintbrushes, slinging bits of paint at each other. One of the boys took the brush and drew it down Gilbert's face from his forehead past his mouth.

A few days later Gilbert got sick. We called Dr. Steele and he examined him and said he had rheumatic fever. He grew consistently worse until finally we called another doctor whom we knew had more experience. He examined Gilbert and told us he did not have rheumatic fever but we had better hurry him to a hospital. We immediately took him to Bluefield. There was no bed for him in the children's ward so they put him in a big room with several men. In retrospect, we figure God had His hand in, for my brother-in-law Fountain Sumner happened to be in the same room. Gilbert knew him well and adapted himself to the situation.

The doctors examined Gilbert very closely and finally determined that he had lead poisoning. I asked where it could have come from. "Have you been painting with lead paint?" Then I remembered the porch. Lesson learned. Gilbert recovered quickly and it is God's blessing that he didn't suffer long-term damage.

As children play, their minds usually are on just what they are doing at any given moment. They pay little attention to their surroundings unless they are warned about some danger. Such was the case with little Gloria. I was away at school in Chicago and Recie was taking care of the children. Gilbert was old enough to do some chores and watch out for his sister but he was elsewhere on the homestead when Recie looked out into the parking lot where Gloria was playing. Recie detected a movement near her. Taking a closer look she saw a snake coiled and ready to strike. She screamed, "Run, Gloria, run!" Fortunately Gloria ran in toward the house instead of toward the snake.

Many times our small ones had croup and colds. Gilbert once had it so bad that when he was laid down he could hardly breathe. We took him up and walked with him with his head on our shoulders. When my children were small and had trouble going to sleep I would gather them up in my arms and start singing to them. One song I used to coax them to slumber was, "Close your sleepy eyes my little buckaroo." I needed the tender love they both gave to us and required from us. In the war, I had been schooled in conflict and it was difficult to adjust to such unconditional love. But I did.

Growing up in the country meant we had to provide not only our own food and shelter but also our medical care. Ever hear of "cauterizing" a wound? Many times in past wars it was the only way to stop the flow of blood. A knife blade would be heated red hot and then slapped on the cut, causing a burn and closing off the blood vessels. Once when I was about sixteen I noticed a huge wart on one of my wrists. Every time I took off my shirt or coat it would drag over the wart and cause it to stay irritated all the time. I got to thinking about cauterizing it and thought to myself that fire is a healer. (I would not recommend the following to anyone now. Back then it was just a matter of doing what you could to get things done.) The wart was about the size of a dime. I got a box of matches and a large needle and went out on the porch where I could see well. I heated the needle and punched it down to where I knew the bottom of the wart was. I did this until I went around the wart twice with the hot needle. Then I went down through the center and made a circle all round the top until I had burned the entire wart. I wrapped a rag around it and the next day it had festered up very badly. I put a bit of clover bloom on it and tied it up again, and by the next day it had begun to shrink. In about three days it was below the surface of the skin and I forgot all about it until one day when I was bathing. I looked at the place where I thought it had been, looked at the other wrist and I showed no sign of the wart. Painful as it was, the fire had done its work.

My cousin Annie Campbell Rinehart writes:

During the Depression folks living far off the beaten path seldom obtained medicine from doctors because most could not afford to pay. They had to make do with home remedies. My dad once had a carbuncle on the back of his neck. It was a sore similar to a boil but much more painful. There was only one Slippery Elm tree on the Rinehart Mountain and dad hated to have to take bark from it, but his pain was so bad he went ahead and cut a slab from the tree. He scraped the inside of the bark and used the sap to make a poultice for the carbuncle. After leaving it on a few days the sore came to a head. Then mom, Aunt Mandy, took a yarn string and slipped it under the core and lifted it out. She bandaged the wound and it soon healed up.

Wilted cabbage or plantain leaves were used for small infections. We placed the wilted leaf over the sore and kept it bandaged a few days to draw out the infection.

For chapped hands and feet we used mutton tallow. It was hard, coarse fat from sheep. Mom melted it and rubbed on our hands and feet. We got mutton tallow from Jim Cook's farm to waterproof my boots.

When we had an upset stomach and were vomiting, mom would brown some corn meal in a skillet and then pour enough water in it to make a pitcher full. She would let it set for a couple of hours, then have us drink a small amount at a time.

Catnip tea was given to young babies for colic. The juice from the horehound plant was used do make candy drops. Crushed jewelweed was used for bee stings, as were tobacco leaves were also used. My dad was a great believer in tobacco leaves for cuts and bruises.

Mustard poultices were used to treat pneumonia. Mom would mix powdered mustard and enough water to make a paste and then spread it with cloth and place the cloth on the person's chest. A window was kept open so that the sick people would have plenty of fresh air.

Dad used a cup of scalded milk with a few sprinkles of black pepper as a sleep aid.

A laxative was made with sap from walnut bark. Granny Whitt would mix the sap with some water and boil it down to a gooey subsistence. She let it cool and used it to make small balls which she called polls.

Granny Whitt also made a medicine from the scrapings of wild cherry tree bark, some water and a few spoonfuls of moonshine to keep it from spoiling. She called the medicine "bitters" and said it helped her sore side. Asafetida was used for colds and chest congestion. It was a bad smelling resin obtained from various Asiatic plants and used as a medicine. It was placed in a small bag hung around the sick person's neck.

Dr B. W. Steele, of Mullens, sent four people to our home on Rinehart Mountain to be cured of tuberculosis. Joe Whitt and two of his children, Okey and Opal came and stayed all summer. Years later Lorena McComas came for the summer. Dr. Steele gave them strict rules to follow. They had to eat six raw eggs a day. Mom stirred them up in milk and flavored it with vanilla. They needed fresh air day and night and Joe slept out on the porch. They were ordered to get out in the sunshine every day, get plenty of rest, eat lots of fresh vegetables, and drink plenty of milk. All of them lived long and productive lives.

In addition to making their own medicines, mountaineers were also skilled at making their own alcoholic beverages. "Moonshiners" were very common in the mountains as I was growing up. The law, to be sure, was very serious about catching them and putting them out of business, but stills and homebrew could be hidden anywhere in the mountains. The stillers always tried to pick a secluded place in a deep ravine or hollow, where smoke would not be detected. The presence of moonshiners provoked excitement in some, misery in others, and sublime pleasure for many.

One day in late fall when all the foliage had turned I was in the woods looking for the tough kinds of weed that grew long and straight. They made perfect arrows for my home made bow. Sometimes I could shoot them with the wind and they would soar a great distance, and I derived a lot of pleasure from this self-made sport. As I trudged the woods I stumbled on a sack full of half-gallon fruit jars. I took the sack home and gave it to my mother. When she asked where I got it I just told her I found it. Evidently the jars were from the moonshiners who may have forgotten, in their drunken stupor, where they left them.

5

Appalachia

CITY FOLK CAN NEVER FULLY appreciate what it means to be close to the land, as many West Virginians are and as our family has always been. Being outdoors may mean a hunting trip or a day of fishing, while others just take a leisurely drive in the country. On two separate occasions I chose to spend a day with my two sons back where I grew up in Cedar Creek, in Wyoming County. My youngest son was born after we left the farm there, but we went to places where as a youth I had helped my dad with the crops and picked blackberries and huckleberries. He wanted to know how it was as I grew up during the Depression. I told him some of the things our parents did in order to cope, how my mother picked wild greens to eat. He had many questions. We climbed to the highest point in the area and sat for a long time, looking at the ragged results of strip mining.

I went back with my older son in early spring, when the leaves were just beginning to fill out. The forest floor was covered with wildflowers. Out in the wilderness, away from the smoke and fumes of cars and trains, they seemed to grow much bigger than along the well-traveled ways.

We were far enough away from the railway and highway so that there were no sounds other than the gentle wind blowing through the tree tops. Many birds were singing. I invited my son to sit with me on a log and just listen. I turned on my tape recorder and recorded about ten minutes of nature at her finest. Amid the unspoiled beauty and quiet, we enjoyed a very meaningful time together, there on the hillside near where I grew up.

Mountaineers have always fought negative stereotypes. CBS television once proposed a reality show transplanting a family from Appalachia to Beverly Hills. This otherwise insulting idea could be interesting. Why not encourage them to do this, but make it a level playing field and send a family from Beverly Hills to live in the mountains? The families could trade lives and video the result. Both families would take only toiletry articles and a few personal items. Otherwise they would use whatever clothing was found in each respective closet, whatever food is in the pantry, whatever mode of transportation is available.

Saturday evening prime time would be a good time slot for such a show. We already know how a hillbilly would fare in the city by "The Beverly Hillbillies." West Virginians' toughness, creativity, and closeness to the land would serve them well in any context. As for the maiden with the pig tails, overalls and straw hat, our own Mountaineer - with his long rifle and buckskins - would have rescued that damsel, if indeed she was in distress. But how about the Beverly Hills family moving into the mountains? How would they fare?

The word Appalachia may first bring to mind the mountain range, but for many years the Appalachian chain was thought of as a wilderness, home to low-wage earners, illiterate farmers, coal miners, blue-collar workers. Appalachia's nine states are all rich in natural resources— coal, timber, natural gas, and water. West Virginia is the only state totally within Appalachia. I was born and raised in West Virginia and after my service in World War II I couldn't wait to return to these mountains I love. I married a coal town girl and raised my children here, where they could be close to their grandparents. Under their influence my sons and daughter learned many of the simple ways of life, and learned to be comfortable with and respectful of not only the elderly but their peers as well. And they learned to treat the environment as it should be treated.

What has Appalachia contributed to the nation as a whole? Many West Virginians still descend into the earth, extracting the rich bituminous coal to fire the furnaces that warm homes in many other states. In the last century we provided the energy needed to build a war machine unmatched in the history of the world, to defeat those who attacked our nation and who would control the entire world. That machine was built with the blood and bones of many a coal miner who died in the darkness of the mines. The fate of the free world literally hinged on the hard work of Appalachians.

It has been interesting to read Senator Byrd's speeches about the advance of coal research. The future of coal in West Virginia seems to still be of great interest to him. Both the mine workers' union and coal operators agree that this research should be an ongoing and will prove beneficial to the economy as a whole, since coal is our primary economic base. Without proper research and advancement, production and use of coal will dwindle and our state will be left without an industry. (Given the drastic loss of mining jobs over the past fifty years, it's looking more like that now.)

I have a Beckley newspaper clipping dated July 23, 1983. The article, "Must think of new ways to use coal," was filled with information about everything that   can be made

One of my first jobs, on a work crew near Montgomery.

from coal. It showed a "coal tree" diagram listing the hundreds of products that can, with proper research, be made from coal—things that could be exported or consumed locally. The article argued that diversified economies do not just happen, they have to be cultivated.

The author argued that we must show others we are guiding our destiny rather than blindly following it.

Considering the state's economy at the time, and the drastic loss of mining jobs as a result of mechanization, I thought that West Virginia might finally come of age. I also thought how interesting it would be to save this article and see, a decade or two down the road, what progress had been made. I put the clipping in my scrap book.

After reading a recent speech by Senator Byrd, I got the clipping out and read it again. Here we are, 25 years down the road and the talk of research and advancement is still mostly talk. This is a good time to challenge our leaders about this. How long will it be until they realize that we in the Mountain State really do need to diversify our economy and move on? We read in the papers and hear on the news of so many millions being spent to research this and study that, and you'd think that after all this research and study something valuable for our state would emerge. Meanwhile, we wait.

When West Virginia's played-out coalmines began to shut down forty years ago, the out-of-state owners of the mineral rights left our little coal towns to fend for themselves. These absentee owners provided no help in building better roads or sewage treatment plants or replacement industries. Most coal camps are too small to incorporate so as to better compete for government money. Helen, where we lived for almost fifty years, is not incorporated. We do not have elected officials, so we depend on advice and help from any and all sources. Senator Byrd must be aware of the kind of help we need here in our effort to enhance the Coal Heritage Trail. One effort at Helen is to establish a rest area where folks can stop and rest and learn about coal mining and coal camp life as it was before mechanization eliminated so many jobs and a way of life.

When Mr. Byrd's name appears in the media saying he has been able to add x number of dollars to the many projects that bear his name, we are proud of his record. However, we need him to remember where he started out. We would like to be able to say Senator Byrd helped us establish sewage systems, clear the obstructions in our streams that cause flooding, helped us clean up our streams and cut through EPA red tape. (Up in Ury, a small town a mile north of Helen and well known to Senator Byrd, the citizens want to change the course of Winding Gulf creek a few feet so their property will not continually flood. But they're forbidden to do so.) When we appeal to our local officials for help and advice their excuse is always that money is tight; yet the officials' names keep rolling out when millions go to other areas. Those may be important, but those of us in the rural areas feel left out. Appalachia was essential to our winning World War II, as were the coal miners who died in the darkness or contracted Black Lung or were maimed in the effort to keep our factories open and running with the coal they mined. The memory of these older miners should be respected via the restoration of the towns they lived and worked in.

The reality is just the opposite. When the coal companies or loggers pull out of an area, they do not leave any infrastructure to support the workers in their later years. Instead, they leave towns without sewage treatment facilities and in many cases without suitable drinking water. Dilapidated buildings sit empty and rot away, becoming constant eyesores to passersby.

We need you, Senators. As small towns we do not have the ability to do this on our own. We are trying, but we need your help.

I believe the future of Appalachia depends on her natural resources, and the time will come when our leaders will come to value what can still be found in these beautiful mountains. A hundred years ago our pristine creeks, rivers and lakes teemed with fish and our hills were full of game. However, in recent years, as strip mining has evolved into the abominable practice of removing entire mountaintops, many hundreds of our creeks and rivers have simply disappeared. (I hasten to say I have no negative feelings for the workers who must make a living with this kind of work; I have great respect for any who labor to support their family.)

But it has always been a mystery to me why our elected officials allow this to happen, while the profits from our natural resources flow entirely out of state. Why have no factories been built in our area to make furniture

Reverend Dewey Wilson and friends at Helen Baptist Church.

from our abundant hardwoods? Why do we not have clean-burning power plants here, so we can sell—rather than give—our power to surrounding states? Our political and business leaders should provide a simple answer to these questions.

The Tamarack Center in Beckley showcases the state's many artists and craftspeople. While I don't object to the name, I have always wondered about it. If the tamarack tree has contributed to the state economy, past or present, I can't find any evidence for it. The tamarack is a member of the pine family and typically grows in Canada and New England. It can be found only in the very northernmost part of West Virginia. Many other trees have proven to be much more useful to the state. When I was growing up it was the job of my brother and I to go up the mountain and cut a back log for the fireplace. My dad told us to bring home either hickory or oak, both of which lasted for a week in the fireplace. He never mentioned a tamarack. The chestnut tree also played a key role in the settlement of our mountains, providing both food and lumber. Old homes had puncheon floors made from the stately chestnut tree. No other tree has provided as much for the state as this old tree. Something should be named after the chestnut, the hickory, the oak. A tamarack may be a fine tree, but until the Tamarack Center was built a lot of us wouldn't have known whether to shoot at one or climb it or catch it with a baited trap.

But not all of us are craftspeople or artists. As coal is depleted, what value can be placed on this area of historically low wage earners? A self-sustaining, post-mining community is slowly becoming a reality in Helen, a coal camp south of Beckley on Route 16. We lived there from 1956 until 2006. The younger folk of the town are taking an interest in making the town look better so it may become a stopping place along the historic Coal Heritage Trail. But that will not happen until the powers that be take a greater interest in miners, those still in the industry and those long retired or dead, and realize nothing can be accomplished without help from the state.

We see and hear a lot about how the congress will not pass an energy bill. The current President would like to tap into the oil reserves in Alaska. The objections are that the wilderness should be preserved. That position is ironic indeed, for the coal companies and logging companies are tearing our beautiful mountains apart. Our pristine wilderness is no longer, as huge scars disfigure our treeless mountaintops and our valley streams are clogged with refuse. Every day one can find a new announcement detailing where the companies will be stripping, valley filling, and logging.

Again, I am not bitter toward the men and women who make their living in these industries. What galls me are the strippers and loggers and mine owners who show total disregard for the welfare of the people they leave behind, the mess they make, and most of all the helplessness of the towns and individuals to prevent the flooding that follows the logging and mountaintop removal.

Our own of Helen is a prime example, having suffered through numerous floods in recent years. We have no political base from which to launch inquiries and log our problems. We are, however, beginning to stir. We have organized The Winding Gulf Restoration organization (WGRO). It's pronounced just as what it means: We Grow.

One resource we West Virginians have in abundance may soon be more valuable than the oil flowing from the foreign countries where our men and women now wage war. We cannot drink oil; we cannot eat the refuse piles left to dam our streams and rivers. But our Appalachian mountains are full of clean, clear streams of water. Water, the one natural resource over which man has no control other than to pollute it. Someday our clean water may be more valuable than our coal.

The Bible describes the cycle of water as it rains onto our land and flows into our streams and through our bodies. The rivers run into the sea, yet the sea is not full; to the place from which the rivers come, there they return again. As a nation we need to look closely at the rivers and creeks that run through Appalachia, and treat them with care. Our goal should be to restore them to the pristine, life-giving conditions in which we first found them. Our lives may depend on it.

Loggers and huge earth movers disfigure the mountain tops, but unfortunately too many West Virginians do no respect the land, either, dumping their personal refuse on the hillsides or out their car windows. I have talked with many people not only close to home but all over the county, and the question is always the same: "Why isn't something being done about the litter problem?" The answer is always the same: They can't seem to find out who is guilty.

Well, let's narrow it down. The governor doesn't throw down litter. The members of the legislature don't throw it down. The sheriff and other local authorities don't do it. So if it isn't any of them, it must be us! So, what are WE going to about it? Let's all start with the governor and ask all the elected leaders to fix it so people who live a long way from landfills can get rid of large pieces of refuse more easily. Other states provide the means to do this. Many of our of citizens pay for garbage hauling, but there is no plan for used appliances and other large items. Unless WE do something, the litter problem is here to stay, and we will remain stuck with it, for it's obvious that none of our elected officials has the political will to do anything about it. Evidently, it remains for us to police each other, if need be.

If you see me throw something out of my car window, honk three times. If I see you do it, I will honk three times. I can see a time when thousands of automobiles all over the state will be honking. Loud and clear.

6

The Working Life

A FTER MY MILITARY SERVICE MY civilian life began with various kinds of labor before I settled into the coal mines. As with my five years of military life, the thirty-five years of coal mining dominate my memories. Occasionally still my time at war and my time at hard work in the mines invade my dreams as one, or a small news item will trigger the memory of one or both. School days, memories of old Sunday School teachers, patrols and bombers, fighters, cannon, mortars, machine gun fire, and Nambu gun sounds run their gamut.

But this old veteran busies himself with at hand tasks. My mind travels an old veteran's life, from boyhood to school to riding the rails to pounding steel for a construction company and cutting right of way for power companies. These flash through my mind daily. Sometimes the cracking timbers of the coal mine mingle with the blast of seventy-five millimeter cannon fire, to the ominous roar of the one-fifty-fives. Ships at sea lobbing eighteen-inch shells into the September darkness of the jungle. The changing of the guard, the changing of the foliage and all its colors mingling into glory. The jungle remains hot, green, lush and dangerous, and the coal mine cool, dark and sometimes quiet. When I would work a shift alone repairing a machine sometimes the only sound I heard was the occasional crack of a breaking timber or the hiss of methane escaping a coal seam.

I established in my first two books that coal mining is one of the most challenging and dangerous occupations in the U.S. I recall that an insurance salesman came to our home on Cedar Creek. He had almost completed an application for me when he asked what I did in the mine. When I told him I was an underground electrician he just folded up the paper and said he could not insure me, for I was in the most dangerous occupation in America at the time.

In the mine where I worked at Otsego we were mining out a section which involved what we commonly called a mountain ride. The top just slowly settled. To support the roof it was necessary to set the timbers closer and closer together over time until finally there was barely room to crawl out of the section. The top had sagged down very close to the belt line, which carried both miners and coal into and out of the mine. At quitting time one man would volunteer to ride the belt out and if he made it he would stop and start the belt as a signal, and we would all climb on. Mere inches separated us from the settling top. Many times I would compare conditions in the mine with combat situations. It is miracle I survived on both counts.

Mining work carries much irony and tragedy for the men and women who perform it. When I was the recording secretary of local union 6195 at Otsego I prepared many retirement papers for older miners who had been deprived of the education needed to fill out the forms and plow through the red tape. Other times I just had to sign the papers for them in my official capacity. The latter was the case with one Tom Kellum who lived at Glen Rogers. He had completed all the paperwork and submitted it to me, and I had forwarded it to the UMWA. He was ready. All he had to do was inform the company of his intent to retire. He finished out the current month and along with a foreman entered the mine at Otsego. Since he was the pumper it was part of his job to go into a worked-out region of the mine to check his pumps. The rail track into the mine was, as in all coal mines, low in some places and high in others. One low place always had six to eight inches of standing water. When a motorman came to this low place he merely pulled down the trolley pole and drifted through the water hole. (A trolley pole connects directly to the high-voltage wires that power the motor.) As momentum carried the motor up the other side he would put the trolley pole back in place, never turning off the controls.

On this day, as Tom and the motorman passed through the standing water, and the latter took down the trolley pole. He was unaware that a pocket of deadly methane gas had gathered above them. When he put the pole back on the trolley line the sparks ignited the methane. Both Tom and the foreman were instantly smothered in flame. The foreman had terrible burns to his face and both his ears were burned off. He escaped with his life but lived with these scars the rest of his days.

Tom went into a coma, where he remained for a full month. He never regained consciousness and died on what was to be his last day of work in the coal mine.

I wonder what he wanted to do with the rest of his life? Certainly a life of retirement, as I can attest, may have had a profound and healthful effect on him, but sadly he was denied this by the rigors of his chosen profession.

While watching the media report the tragic loss of men in a Utah coal mine, I recall when cave-ins were a regular occurrence at our own mines. Our instincts and experience advanced to the point that we could read the mountain and tell by its ominous sound that it was coming down, and we ran for cover. Sometimes we engaged in what is commonly called Russian Roulette. One morning as we came toward the surface in a jeep we suddenly noticed small rocks falling from the ceiling, following a previous slate fall about t thirty feet high and fifty feet long. We all got out of the jeep and waited a few minutes. When no more rock fell one man got into the jeep, backed it up several feet and went full speed through the dangerous part. Then as we waited again and nothing fell, we ran across one at a time, very fast.

Similarly, as the daily run of Japanese planes came over Guadalcanal, we instinctively learned to take cover, though there was very little in the way of hiding places. In the mines, we could more or less control the falling mountain by cribbing up a place to make it break when it fell. On Guadalcanal, little holes could protect you from shrapnel but provided no cover for a direct hit. The bombs usually left a crater in the soft sandy soil of the island about twenty feet across and ten to fifteen feet deep. When I think of those craters my thoughts lead me to also think of a well I dug at our home in Cedar Creek, the difference being that one hole had many wiggletails in it while the other drew fresh, clean water from a coal seam along the creek.

One of the jobs I had in general labor was on the supply gang. As the name implies, supplies of any kind needed by the two production shifts was delivered into the mine by the supply gang. I worked this for about a year. Transferring of supplies was physically challenging, and many methods of making it easier were tried and rejected. Finally, we hit on a simple method: Simply sit on the spill plate, put your feet over on the other side of the belt and transfer the timbers and such by grasping the front end and guiding t hem onto the other belt. Necessity is still the motherhood of invention, and still, it was hard and dangerous.

In my mining gear, long after my mining days were over.

My last effort at formal schooling came a few years after I had been discharged from the Marine Corps. I had few marketable skills, so I knew I needed to further my education if I was to be something more than a general laborer in the coal mine. The mining work I was doing at this time required very little book knowledge, but I knew I needed more. I settled on Coyne Electrical School in Chicago. Practical experience is the best education, of course, but Coyne would teach me to read blueprints, wire motors, and so on. I had to pay for the school myself, my ten-year post-service period under the GI Bill having run out. But that decade after the war had been full of pain and anguish, as I battled with myself and tried to forget what I had been through. A sick man can't focus on learning.

I came home a couple of times for weekend visits and always had to get someone to meet me at the train station either in Bluefield or Prince. The long rides on the train gave me time to reflect on things present, past and future. For the present, I was away from my family, always feeling lonely. I missed them so very much. The feeling of the little ones with their arms around me and the tranquil setting of our meals together were the things I missed the most.

All in all, Coyne lasted twelve weeks and cost me about two thousand five hundred dollars. When I came home we were flat broke. I made good grades but had to cut the schooling short by three weeks because Recie had become ill and I needed to get back to work in the mines and get the hospitalization process going.

I resolved that after returning home I would never be away from them for an extended period except in emergencies. In retrospect I suppose that is one of the primary reasons I gave little thought to marriage before going into the war. Even in school many times my thoughts were on home and family. I had seen and listened to those who were married and left families behind as they lamented their absence.

After I got work on the maintenance force it become necessary to troubleshoot the high voltage lines. Sometimes it was a simple blowout, easily found. Other times it was a simple short circuit between the line and ground, which required the current to jump only a fraction of an inch to trip the big breakers. One old-timer told me, "Son, look for a flea, not an elephant." The advice came in handy. Once, several crews had spent many hours trying to find the trouble. They had examined the line and saw no sign of a short or a blowout. I went back to where I had started my shift and began a slow, systematic search for anything out of the ordinary. Cleaning the cable with a rag inch by inch was slow but necessary. Finally I came upon what I was looking for, a small brown spot on the cable about t he size of a nickel. Not much of a sign, but I mashed on the spot with my finger and it was soft. I knew I had found the trouble. Instead of blowing a hole through the outer insulation of the cable the force of the short split the wiring inside each way a couple of inches. Sure enough, it proved to be a flea instead of an elephant.

These days, I still find it essential to work. Even at my age, I work in my shop for a half day almost every day. Tools can fool people—they hook up a piece of equipment and if it doesn't perform according to their expectations they are disappointed. But the rule of thumb is, work the tool, don't let it work you. Most of my experience with tools goes back to my youth. I have already covered in *Coal Bloom* many of the simple tools of yesteryear. We see them now mostly in antique shops and flea markets and on display at museums and most youngsters have no idea what they are. I wonder, as I flip the switches that bring my power tools to life, how the old ones coped with the rigors of hand-making everything they needed. But then again, I think, they were not in the hurry we are today. Where did they have to go? All they had to do was make the most of each day. They made what they could and finished it tomorrow.

In my own workshop you might see an assortment of tools dating back more than three quarters of a century. A level hangs on a nail, an old paint scraper with removable blade lies on the bench, and an array of sockets and ratchets are laid out in a red tool box. Over the years I have gathered tools to accomplish most any job I choose to do. I recently passed on to my sons the claw hammer and drawing knife that belonged to my father, himself a carpenter.

Some may wonder why an old-timer like me would go out to his shop every morning for several hours. I have no appointments, no schedule to keep, no important things I must do. Rather, the events of my life, and the emotions I must deal with, compel me to be alone with this hobby. I stay busy working with wood both in my shop and inside the house.

My son in law Ralph and I have been building little ten-inch replicas of the old country outhouses. They have become very popular and sales are brisk. Ralph gets old weathered lumber from his decaying oak fence and I trim it down with my planer.

Also, we hold a huge family reunion every July and as it approaches I think about what to make to auction off there. I primarily do these things to keep my mind and body busy.

My home is dense with mementoes of my life. The walls all display my handiwork, and all through the house are little reminders that trigger memories. I see a moment from the darkness of the coal mine and hear the cracking of timbers, the thunderous roar of the mountain filling in the vacant space left by the removed coal.

Some of my tools were used to repair mining equipment and many still have traces of grease and grime left from working in the black coal mud. My old turning lathe, bought in 1948, is now obsolete and I must make parts for it myself as they wear out. My table saw, now more than two decades old, still enables me to make lumber from raw timber. I recycle old wood and take pleasure in the beautiful grain when it's finished into picture frames and such.

The time I take for myself this way keeps my mind away from the thunder of sixteen-inch cannon fire and the roar of bombs. I lose myself in the measurement of the wood and find comfort in knowing I'm still using tools I used as a mechanic/electrician for many decades. As my hands are busy, my mind is working, sometimes overtime, as I make something for the grandchildren or the children to hang on their wall and remind them of me long after I have departed this earth. They will say, My daddy made this, my grandpa made this.

In addition to hand tools, my typewriter and now computer have given me a great deal of pleasure. I have been fortunate to place my first two books in various shops, including the Little Red Brick House gift shop in Beckley. My son Gilbert had his twin grandchildren with us and as they roamed the book section the twins came upon copies of my two books. "Hey, that's Grandpa Miller!" one shouted.

I take a great deal of pleasure at them recognizing me as an author.

7

Faith

IN THINKING BACK OVER MY life, I have observed that
spirituality rises in proportion to national disasters.
During the Great Depression, more people seemed
interested in church matters, and the same was true of
World War II. As a Marine I did not profess any particular
creed, only that I believed in God. When I attended
different churches or services in peoples' homes, I was
always impressed with the welcome I got. They always
seemed pleased that a member of the armed services would
attend such a meeting. The question always at the forefront
of any faith-based group is this: Exactly how tolerant are
we with those of another persuasion? This brings to mind
an incident I witnessed during the dark days of battle on
Guadalcanal.

One Sunday, during a lull in the fighting, there were two
groups of men engaged in worship, one Catholic and the
other Protestant. A priest and chaplain conducted worship
services for the respective groups. But the next Sunday
there was only one religious leader there to serve both

groups. Only years later did I realize what I had witnessed there in the jungle. When we assess our relationship to God in these modern times, our tolerance is still a question, is it not? The spiritual attitude of an individual, a family, or a community encourages peace and harmony regardless of creed.

Our little town of Otsego had churches to serve both the black and white community. The drought of the 1930's was a serious threat to all and one day a group of fine African American ladies from Otsego decided to have a special prayer meeting to pray for rain. The day wore on, hot, humid and very uncomfortable for all. As they began to gather at the church they all looked askance at this one lady who had an umbrella tucked under her arm. They questioned her about being foolish. Her reply was simple and to the point: "What is we gonna pray for?"

A black lady I knew was the school cook at Otsego grade school and the common-law wife of a man well-known and liked by all. Another man decided he would take the cook lady away from her first live-in. He did so, and they lived together as common law partners until he passed away. It was decided that a black minister from Mullens would preach his funeral. He also worked at Otsego and knew the pair and the situation under which they lived, which was very controversial to the Bible. The minister also knew that everyone in the congregation knew the couple.

It was a salt and pepper gathering, as there were as many white folk attending the funeral as there were black. The minister rose and positioned himself behind the coffin. He stood there for long minutes before uttering a word. The congregation eagerly awaited his message, one, they thought, that would dwell on the sins of humanity. At long last he began to speak. He pointed down to the man in the coffin and asked, "Where is de man?" He pointed to himself. "*I* don't know where he is." He pointed at the congregation. "And *you* don't know where he is. Only *God* know where he is." He went on with his sermon and put the man neither in heaven nor in hell. He paused now and then and repeated his question. "Where is de man? *I* don't know and *you* don't know. Only *God* know where he is." It was an interesting experience for me, for I had heard many sermons preached at funerals for people whom I knew were not Christian. This humble and uneducated minister taught me more about how to be humble myself, and let God be the judge.

There was a beer joint adjacent to the African American church in Otsego, and they tried in vain to shut it down, with no help from politicians. They held a prayer meeting and prayed for God to remove this blight on their Christian efforts. The next morning the beer joint was just a pile of ashes. One of the ladies was heard to say, "Some time de Lawd need a little help."

She had slipped over in the dead of night and torched the place.

8

The Land Down Under

ABOUT TEN YEARS AGO I was contacted by an Australia World War II researcher named Rob Crawford, after he saw a piece I published in the Guadalcanal Echoes newsletter. He has made it his life-long avocation to search out many of the artifacts and traces of the war in the Pacific and help remember America's protection of his home islands. His number one passion was the battle of Guadalcanal, in which I played a role, as described in my earlier books. His quest led him on several trips to the Solomon Islands and elsewhere in the South Pacific. It was exactly eight months to the day after the "Day of Infamy" that America's first offensive action against the empire of Japan was launched at Guadalcanal. This was the first rung of the ladder of islands that extended all the way up to Japan. These islands were among the many that played such a crucial part in stopping Japan from its conquest of Australia, New Zealand and wherever their zeal would next take them.

Historians looking back now realize what a turning point Guadalcanal was for not only Australia and New Zealand, but for the entire war. Wikipedia (see the full article in the Appendix) summarizes it this way:

> *The Guadalcanal campaign was costly to Japan strategically and in material losses and manpower. Roughly 30,000 Japanese troops were killed during the campaign. Japan lost control of the Solomons Islands and the ability to interdict Allied shipping to Australia. Japan's major base at Rabaul was now directly threatened by Allied air power. Most importantly, scarce Japanese land, air, and naval forces had disappeared forever into the Guadalcanal jungle and surrounding sea. The Japanese aircraft and ships destroyed and sunk in this campaign were irreplaceable, as were their highly-trained and veteran crews. It thus can be argued that this Allied victory was the first step in a long string of successes that eventually led to the surrender of Japan and the occupation of the Japanese home islands.*

I lost track of Rob but my son David recently reestablished contact with him. It's a real blessing to know such a man as Rob. His son, age eleven, did a school speech about the war in the Pacific and received a standing ovation. (I wish I had a copy of that speech.) My link to the people of Australia is still strong, and the land will retain a special place in my heart, for they were a grateful nation, along with New Zealanders. America's first offensive against the empire of Japan was meant to insure that Japan would not overwhelm these South Pacific friends. The people of both countries welcomed us with open arms and opened their homes to us.

Few Americans had heard of the Solomons before World War II. Courtesy Australian Travel and Tourism Board.

There were many facets of life in Australia I regret not taking advantage of. These people knew how valuable our entrance into the Pacific theater was to them, for they had no powerful military with which to battle the Nippon war machine. My memories of these two countries will linger not only in me but on the pages of my books. Readers will learn about a simple mountain man and his memories of how it was "back yonder a ways," and how he travelled halfway around the world to defend a small island, and so defend his country.

In a letter to the author, Rob writes, "I can't tell you how many people I've talked to who know nothing about Guadalcanal, Savo Island, or The Slot. In my endeavor to learn more about Australia's role in World War II, I became obsessed with what happened in '42 in the Solomon Islands. If the Yanks had not fought and held the islands, of course, I wouldn't be here now. How many American men gave their lives so that the people of Australia would be safe? That's worth remembering, worth talking about, and they did not die in vain."

Interestingly, four years after the battle of Guadalcanal and two years since Japan surrendered, the last Japanese soldier surrendered. He was captured while breaking into the Honiara Police compound to steal food. He had a water bottle, a broken Australian bayonet, and a Japanese entrenching tool. Rob adds: "I also have some friends on Guadalcanal that gave me approximate coordinates of several Japanese stragglers hiding near Mt. Makarakomburu. [Highest peak in Solomon Islands, 2,447m.] I have heard little recently about stragglers, the last time being 2001. A friend of mine who is a local customs authority claims some villagers had being supplying a straggler with medicine and clothes, blankets etc, but respect his wishes not to be found. Particularly by Japanese."

Rob Crawford also very kindly sent me something I never thought I would see again: Sand from the beach at Guadalcanal.

It is only a small glass jar about four inches tall and one and a half inches in diameter, but looking at it brought back many things I have tried for sixty-six years to forget. But I can forget very few things about that time, for the images are embedded in my memory so deeply that the mere mention of these islands, where my life changed forever, brings them back immediately.

In Australia.

The boats had left their rendezvous area, where the ships made slow circles in the sea, and now stood in a straight row at the line of departure. Two regiments stood abreast on the boats a few yards apart as the ships began their journey toward the shining sandy beach.

At first the land described only a small line of brown against the green of the dense jungle. The line became ore more jagged as we drew closer. Invariably some boats fell behind. The acceleration of the boats brought the beach closer and it loomed much wider than we thought at first. As the boats drew closer to the landfall some men made the sign of the cross, some bowed in silent prayer, and others just stared ahead at the unknown. No one knew what the next few minutes would bring.

Low on the port side the sergeant felt the bottom of the boat scrape the sandy soil. Previous training had made us adept at unloading and he threw himself over the side. His platoon followed.

The first sand was under several inches of water and our footing was unsure. As our feet struggled onto dry sand, the crunching and slipping was nearly drowned out by the roar of the Higgins boats as they hurried to leave the beach and return the boats to the relative safety of the sea, beyond the land artillery and mortar we supposed the enemy to have installed beyond the beach.

Gaining traction I hurried up the beach and toward the jungle's edge.

I waited. Waited for oncoming fire that never came. The landing itself was unopposed. But the sand of Guadalcanal began almost immediately to etch its grit into the body and soul of every man who landed. The sand was to remain in and on us for many days.

The rest of that day, August 7, 1942, was calm, as we unloaded ammo and part of the food supply. The loose and shifting sand made walking with a load difficult but by day's end much had been accomplished.

The next day, August 8, we took the landing strip the Japanese had been building, renaming it Henderson Field. But that day also brought Japanese bombers from Rabaul. Our precious ships were in much danger, so U.S. Rear Admiral Richmond K. Turner made the decision to pull out before the bombers could inflict greater damage—even though less than half the food and other supplies we'd need had been unloaded.

On Guadalcanal D-Day +3 the sea was vast and empty. There were no American ships to boost morale, no planes in the sky to ward off the bombers and fighters which would come at Noon every day. The Japanese bombed and strafed at will, as I described at length in *War and Work*.

Needless to say, we were preparing ourselves for another Wake Island, another Bataan, as we were apparently another helpless, stranded group, left to its own meager resources.

By night we began to see flashes of light faraway out to sea, followed by crashing sounds we knew could not be the thunder of a natural storm.

The Japanese navy managed to sneak up on part of our fleet and through the night a terrible duel ensued off the coast. We lost four valiant ships, the U.S. cruisers Astoria, Quincy, and Vincennes and the Australian cruiser Canberra, along with their entire crews. Those ships and their brave crews sank to rest on the sandy ocean floor of Iron Bottom Bay. These were the charter members of the "Lost fleet of Guadalcanal."

Throughout August the enemy landed more and more troops until we were outnumbered and outgunned. We were expendable, still more losses in the war that claimed so many. The Japanese soldiers came in droves but were met with fierce resolve, and hundreds lay dead on the sand. Their bodied decomposed where they lay until a dozer came and covered them.

But the sand of Guadalcanal now held the smell of death. Maggots crawled everywhere and now we fought off green flies while trying to eat a spoonful of weevil-infested rice. But since the transport ships had been able to leave us only a few days' worth of food, even with what we captured from the Japanese food was scarce. Dysentery, malaria, fungus, and other jungle maladies began to thin our ranks.

We fought a savage battle far up the Matanikau River and we stood on its banks, where our perimeter had been expanded. The water was clear and pristine looking so we filled our canteens.

The next day a tropical storm came up and the river swelled almost out of its banks. Along with other debris came the bloated bodies of Japanese soldiers who had died in the battle. Their bodies would swirl momentarily on the sand spit of the river and lay there moving gently back and forth until another wave came and washed them out to sea.

On Guadalcanal. U.S. Marine Corps archives.

The monsoons set in. Before the rain the torrential wind swept up the sand and blew it into our eyes. Japanese bombers came again and their ordnance gouged ten-foot deep craters. The craters filled with water, and the water filled with wiggletails. The sand was difficult to climb but we filled our canteens and drank, wiggletails and all.

The sand along the beach had sections of small bushes which allowed us to move unseen, but the hot sand and one hundred and ten degree heat made it difficult to move without standing up for a breath of air now and then.

We sailed away from the Island of Death on December 9, and a look back at these islands showed them as we had first glimpsed them. Savo Island still stood defiant. The green hell of the jungles still looked as beautiful as ever from afar. The sand still gleamed. Man's war could not destroy the raw beauty of God's nature.

9

Spring

MARCH BORROWS A FEW DAYS from April and pays us back in May or June, and April brings a burst of color here and there. Today, as I write this in the cool of evening, I heard again the call of the whippoorwill. It had been some time since I had heard the clear call of this bird, and it set me thinking again of the past. I recalled the conversation I had with my mother about the whippoorwill's first call of the spring, as I related in *Coal Bloom*. In those Depression days the women of small farms did many chores unknown to today's modern woman. True, women today are challenged in many ways these elder women could never have imagined. But the many inventions meant to reduce the housewives' woes and worries have not saved them time or given them more leisure as promised.

The clear and vivid call of the whippoorwill reminds me of my mother in the wood yard. In those days we would drag logs, stumps or anything that would make fire wood and cut them up with a double bit axe. (This is the source of the expression "let the chips fall where they may" and indeed the wood yard was covered with chips. They lay in the sun and dried to the point that merely striking a match to them would ignite them.) In my mind's eye I see my mother with her gingham apron pulled up to form a sack where she gathered the chips. She was adept not only at cooking but she was able and ready to kindle fires, hoe corn, plant a garden, pick wild greens, or do any other farm chore that needed to be done.

In the old days April meant a lot of activity. Planting some crops, getting the ground ready for others. It was also a time when I began to listen. The sounds of spring are unlike any other. Streams were full, fish were jumping, and all over the land was the sound of singing birds, of life bursting through the ground, silently seeking its place in the sun. I also listen for the whippoorwill. I recall one morning after I had been sick with flu that I was stirring the gravy for mom. I was still recovering from the illness but was able to be up and at a few chores. I was still very weak and remember starting to fall, but her hands caught me and guided me away from the hot stove to the wood box at the back of the old cook stove. The whippoorwill again reminded me of her promise: "Thurman, when you hear the first whippoorwill of spring you will not have to get up and build the fire in the cook stove each morning."

Sometimes when I was just a youngster the ice in Cedar Creek began to break up in early spring and the warm sunny days brought a desire to swim. We played "backout" and backed each other out to go swimming in the icy waters. We had to push pieces of ice out of the way to swim. We didn't swim long, mind you, but just wanted to say we had done it, and that was enough to brag about.

April and May are the months for planting root crops and I remember it as time for the "taters" both Irish and sweet. The distinction between the two is in the planting and harvesting. Irish potatoes, or seed potatoes, are cut and quartered into smaller pieces, always sure that at least two "eyes" are in each piece. ("They had to see how to come up," we'd joke.) These potatoes were planted in various ways. Some folk simply dug a trench and spaced the potato pieces about ten inches apart. However, on our farm we always made up hills about three feet apart and placed two small pieces in each hill. This way, when the vines had completely dried up we could easily find the potatoes.

Sweet potatoes, on the other hand, are planted in a different manner, and Dad would see that it was properly done. First, the soil was heaped into a continuous mound about a foot high. When this was accomplished Dad would take his hoe and flatten the top of the ground to about five inches wide. Then he would reverse his hoe and, using the handle, make a trench a couple inches deep. Then it was our job to take buckets to the creek and fill them and carry them back to the mounds and pour the water carefully into the trench. While this went on Dad started placing the potato plants about six inches apart. (Sweet potatoes were put into the trenches as plants, whereas Irish potatoes were actually pieces of the potatoes themselves.) Taking two fingers he made a hole into the wet soil, placed the plant carefully into it, and covered it with dry dirt, leaving two or three inches of the plant above ground.

The process of storing sweet potatoes, however, was altogether different from that of Irish potatoes. I have already described the 'tater hole in *Coal Bloom*. Sweet potatoes are more easily bruised and subject to rot, so in order to preserve them the old farmers would use a large barrel with a layer of sand in the bottom. They would place a layer of sweet potatoes on it and cover that layer with more sand, then more potatoes and so on until the barrel was full. The potatoes were taken out as needed, being careful to always leave the remaining ones separated from each other.

May was also the time to begin harvest season for spring onions, radishes and leaf lettuce. When these matured in early summer we children would go into the coal camp and contract to sell all three of the tasty vegetables. Next morning we would all pitch in and pull them up and make them into small bunches. Then we'd deliver them and collect the money. We brought it to Mom and she in turn used it to buy sugar, salt, lard, and other things we couldn't make for ourselves. The result of our kids' work would eventually grace our dinner table.

May was also the month for checking all our plantings and making sure the proper seeds were sown, but once everything was planted we had a period of relaxation, with more leisure time to play, fish or just loaf. But soon the corn began peeping through the ground and little shoots of life pushed their way up through the warm, moist earth. It wasn't long until we needed to begin first hoeing to keep the weeds from taking over and to give the crops more sunlight. At second hoeing, with the corn a foot high we thinned the hills down to two or three stalks per hill. We likewise hoed the other crops and piled fresh dirt up around them. Then we had another brief period to rest. But on a leased country farm the work goes on constantly with hoeing, weeding, and generally caring for the precious crops upon which we relied to live.

May was always a month of wonder to me as I watched all the trees budding, their brownish colors mingling with the green of the hemlock. Watching Mother Nature put her full force into the beautiful color of spring, the forest ground covered with wildflowers, birds happily flying through the air, adding their beautiful songs to the very special time of new life bursting forth.

On the eighth day of May, 1944, we arrived on the South Pacific island of Pavuvu, awaiting the upcoming roster to be posted telling us who would go home and who must stay and fight. It was my time to come home. On Pavuvu our ranks began to be replenished with fresh new bodies. Young men sought advice from battle-weary veterans of Guadalcanal and New Britain. We did our best to pass on to them whatever we could. Only after they were baptized by the fire of war could any truly understand.

With the rising of the South Pacific tides my mind was filled with the thought that back home the crops are growing, nature is filling the land with the tender green of spring. There on the little island of Pavuvu I stood, ready to rotate home. But where was home? Back in the hills of Appalachia? In a tent city of North Carolina? Could it have been somewhere in the "land down under?" Had the Corps become my home, and was I destined to continue this battle? I did not know. I took stock of my surroundings, looking at myself and the others like me. Energy drained, old before their time. I looked at the fresh new faces of our replacements. I knew before long they too would get old very quickly and their lives would flash before them and they would wonder, Why? Then I thought of Pearl Harbor and knew that they would know, as I did, that their destiny was to quell the evil facing the world on that day.

But now, three years after Pearl Harbor, I stood there on Pavuvu, June 5, 1944, and knew my battle was over. On one side of the world stood one set of warriors, their mission accomplished, their bodies wasted away with no real hope of full recovery. On the other side stood thousands of young faces mingled with the hardened faces of the NCO's and the elder officers, ones who had seen the effects of war time and again. Some young faces were filled with fear, some with mere wondering at what was to come. Some of these new recruits were still in high school when we began our time on Guadalcanal. And on June 6th, D-Day, loomed before all soldiers, but little did they know that in a few short hours so many of their bodies would be strewn over the beaches of Normandy.

On my long voyage back to the states many thoughts filled my mind about what I had endured in my thirty-plus months on the other side of the world. Leaving the Southern Cross and returning to the Big Dipper gave me a feeling of security.

We looked back over the fantail of the ship and Pavuvu receded, finally disappearing, but the image of the island would always be with me. As we stood on deck we saw the great wonders of the ocean depths. Whales came roaring up and blowing, their great tails seemingly waving us farewell, dolphins leaping up and down, sharks circling the fantail.

As our ship sailed for home I tried in vain to dump overboard the agony, the desperation of war. I found out quickly that I could not. The embedded memories were not normal shipboard dunnage. Instead, the memories remained a part of me as I stood on the fantail and watched the ship's wake fade in the distance, just as when I sailed away from the "Island of Death." In the churning wake I saw the faces of my comrades.

As Veterans' Day approaches, there will be many parades and speeches honoring veterans of all our wars. It is good that our nation pauses to do this and to pay tribute to those who gave their lives in combat, those who lost their limbs on the frozen battlegrounds and in the steaming jungles where they fought. Now and then the process should be reversed and tribute paid to the American people and its communities in general. Veterans of the Army, Navy and Marine Corps, should take a drive through the Piney View neighborhood of Beckley. There you will find the names of many streets which are named after the various battles of the South Pacific. Hawaii Avenue, Samoa Drive, New Guinea Avenue, Marshall Street, Midway Road, Kaluha Lane, Fiji Drive, Truk Street, Wake Street, Corregidor Road, New Caledonia Street, Battan Road, Guam Avenue, Tinian Avenue, Saipan Avenue, Iwo Jima Court, Bouganville Avenue, Guadalcanal Avenue, Coral Court. No doubt there are other veterans in my home Raleigh County who were on some of these islands.

When I think of my country, and how much I love it and would sacrifice for it, I think of those who do not share my feelings for it. Much was written about Marc Rich and several other questionable characters

The Southern Cross became a part of the Guadalcanal patch.

receiving pardons at the last minute of President Clinton's term. When Rich—or anyone else—refuses to pay taxes owed to the country, it's a slap in the face of all the people who work low-income jobs but dutifully pay their taxes without complaint. Even more disgusting is that he could be pardoned after he fled to Switzerland and renounced his U.S. citizenship.

This reminds me of another man who declared that he hated the United States and wished he would never hear of it again. "The Man Without a Country" by E.E. Hale recounts the fate of the fictional Phillip Nolan, a former U.S. Army officer who curses the United States during his trial for sedition in 1807. He is sentenced to have his wish fulfilled, and spends the next 56 years of his life at sea and in foreign ports, never seeing or hearing of the United States. After many years Nolan expresses his remorse as he passionately implores a young American sailor to serve his country as she bids him, though the service may carry him through a thousand hells. "No matter what happens to you, no matter who flatters or abuses you, never look at another flag, never let a night pass but you pray God to bless that flag... Stand by her, boy, as you would stand by your own mother." What we remember most of this "man without a country" is his parting words: "Breathes there a man with soul so dead, who never to himself hath said, this is my own, my native land?"

10

Summer

IN JUNE, WE SLIP QUIETLY from spring to summer. Chickens run freely around the place and they'd roost where ever they please. Typical summer thunder comes occasionally, mixing rain and hail.

As I write this, we have had a very dry summer. I have no crops to tend, but I gaze with envy on some of the beautiful gardens here and there. In the August of my years it is not necessary that I grow my own food, as it was when I was young, but I recall gazing with pride on the corn, sweet potatoes, and other vegetables growing taller in field and garden. I thought, I helped bring this about.

In my mind's eye I see my mother out in the potato patch graveling new potatoes to cook with the newly picked half- runner beans. (Graveling is a way of probing into a potato hill to get new potatoes.) Half-runner beans are the opposite of large field beans. She will prepare a full meal from the family garden, having picked a large portion of greens for a salad. She will put it all on the table with a huge pone of hot cornbread. The blessing will be asked and He will be thanked for the bountiful meal. When the fields are full of corn, the beans maturing and the tomatoes large, red and ripe for the eating, it's a happy time around the table. There were no radios, TV's or anything else to distract us from the simple joy of fresh food from our own soil. The hot days of summer would wear on soon enough and as the crops matured and we would begin to lay food by for the winter.

With each change of seasons I am prone to wonder if this will be the last time I will enjoy the tender green of spring, the rustling of the dark green leaves of a storm, or the first gentle fall of a snow flake settling on my cheek. Our family reunion draws ever closer and I wonder about the young ones. Do they know who they are and where they come from? I have covered quite extensively in *Coal Bloom* the lives of my many siblings, only one of which remains other than me. She is from the union of Elvira and Sanford Meadows rather than from Eli Center Miller and Elvira, as I am. I will soon reach eighty-nine and my stepsister Della is halfway through her nineties. The reader may well examine the photos of all my siblings I included in *Coal Bloom* and wonder, Where are their children? Who remains of theirs? Looking down through the long decades I see at once many of them as they were mere babies, watch them grow into adulthood and produce their own offspring until they can now count not only grandchildren but great-grandchildren.

Then there are all the offspring of my many aunts and uncles. Our cousins are legion and scattered to God knows where. I write this just after Memorial Day, and it is memory that makes us give pause to the day. Memorial Day makes me think especially of the four in our family who served in the United States Marine Corps: Russell, Buster (James, also known as Buck), James Vaughn Jr., and myself. Our duties were wide and varied. I think back now and then to the days when Buck, Russell and I wandered in the mountains looking for mountain tea or sarvis berries or just enjoying bring outdoors. I mentioned in one of my writings that we three existed like a tripod. Now they are gone and only I remain. The memories we built in our boyhood days and our times laughing with our siblings provide many thoughts of that carefree time of life. I think about the games and other pastimes we invented and I worry about today's youth, who have so many things provided for them it is difficult for them to choose. I think it is a sad thing for them not to be in touch with nature and her great blessings, as we were.

The summer advances into July and we think again of what this month means to us. We celebrate, we congregate, we cook out and have picnics with family and friends. It's a time of pleasant living. But there is basically no month of the year that does not contain some memory of the war, the mines and where and why I was at a certain place or other.

When I came home from war for a thirty-day furlough Recie and I planned our wedding. There would be no fanfare, no fancy trimmings, for we had determined that a simple wedding was sufficient. The morning of July 30 found us in New Richmond and our old friend Oscar Sparks performed the ceremony.

Recie and I, just married.

Our final wedding anniversary would come six decades later. It similarly came and went with little fanfare except a card from me to Recie. Folks marvel that a couple can stay together sixty-two years, but too many young folks these days can't find a partner willing to make such a long-term commitment. Sad to say, but true.

Back when I was on Guadalcanal Oscar had a son who was also there, in another regiment. He somehow got the news, from I know not where, that I had been killed. He wrote this home to Oscar, who later told me he had agonized over how to break the news to Mom and Dad. But the situation was cleared up before he had to. (I am reminded of Mark Twain's insistence that "News of my demise has been greatly exaggerated.")

The coming of August on the farm found us looking at the tassels atop the cornstalks and realizing it was almost time for cutting and forming shocks and getting ready for winter. Buck and I knew that during the long winter months we would have to carry these shocks to the barn once a week.

As I sit now watching the news this August, I think back to the day the atomic bomb ended the Pacific war. August and September 1945 changed many lives forever. On August 16, 1945, my hometown paper, the Mullens *Advocate*, printed a four-page issue (small because of the newsprint shortage) with headline letters two and a half inches high, in heavy, bold type: "JAPS QUIT; M'ARTHUR BOSS." The story was over twelve column inches and in larger print than the rest of the page and provided details of the Japanese surrender and a picture of Emperor Hirohito. The story informed readers that President Harry Truman had declared a two-day national holiday. The story said, "This official announcement, coming as it did at the end of many hours of waiting and celebration which began early in the morning throughout the world, touched off another celebration which grew in intensity and which dwarfed that of the morning and afternoon."

Just as with Pearl Harbor Day, those of us in the military on that date can pinpoint where we were and what our reactions were when the bomb was dropped on Japan. Much emphasis has been put on gleaning an apology from Japan for its wartime atrocities, and they in turn have sought an apology from the Allies for Hiroshima and Nagasaki. I have written in the past that history has recorded these events and that nothing can change the fact that they happened.

I had already served 28 months in the Pacific at Guadalcanal and New Britain. I came home in the spring of 1944 and was stationed at Camp LeJeune, N.C. My First Marine Division was at that time already busy in Okinawa, and that's probably where I would have been shipped out to first.

Camp LeJeune in the 1940's. U.S. Marine Corps archives.

I had already had all my shots for overseas duty, been examined and requalified for combat, and was packed up and ready to ship out, no doubt to invade Japan, when it was announced that the bomb had been dropped. Recie had already packed to come home and everything was in place so I could leave on a moment's notice.

On that day, when headlines all over the world announced the bombing in huge block letters, we all looked in disbelief. We could not fathom the results at that time. Could it be we would not ship out again? That was the case. As August, 1945, brought the atomic bomb and Japan's surrender, September saw the mustering out of thousands of men and women who had been, as I was, getting ready for the invasion of the mainland of Japan. On September 2, 1945, aboard the Battleship USS *Missouri*, General Douglas MacArthur accepted Japan's complete and unconditional surrender. An exhausted and anxious world watched. On battlefields around the world guns fell silent, heads bowed in prayer. Commanders breathed a sigh of relief at not having to order more men into the breach to be killed or maimed. Mothers stole away to secret places of prayer, and wives anxiously clutched a picture of their husband. If not for the bomb, who knows where I would have been?

September is also memorable for me, as I entered the Marine Corps on September 3, 1940, and five years later, on September 24, was separated from the Corps. The years between provided me with enough memories to write two books, in which I tried my best to paint war as the hell it is.

We set to work rebuilding a nation ravaged by depression and war. Ours was the only nation on earth with the resources to rebuild any country anywhere. We began to put our infrastructure back, built highways, worked in factories, coal mines and steel mills. We built automobiles and homes and businesses.

But as time went on the owners of the mills, factories and businesses began to forget our accomplishment and began sending their work to foreign countries—countries which just a few years before had attempted a forceful takeover of our country.

Many stores sell beach towels made to resemble the American flag. These are taken to the beach and laid on the ground, in great disrespect. I read a story awhile back about a store in Chicago where an American flag was placed on the floor in front of a table where the public could sign their names to some kind of document. I have no objection to the signing of anything, but I do have strong feelings about the flag.

All nations have their own flags and throughout the world these are symbols of their presence. Churches, Boy Scouts, and many other organizations have flags for special occasions. Our own flag was born in a time of turmoil and was hoisted as a sign of freedom. All through our nation, in every little town, a traveler can look around and spot an American flag, and it always indicates where he can find help. He may need a post office, a courthouse or a federal building, and the flag marks all of these. During times of war our soldiers are given flags and told to hoist them after they have taken a hill, an airstrip or other objective. More often than not, this is costly in human lives and sometimes a bullet-ridden, blood-soaked flag is tied to a piece of bamboo or a coconut tree so that all—including the enemy—can see and know that the objective is securely in American control.

Those who place this symbol of liberty on the floor to be trod upon, or to be laid down on a sandy beach, show contempt for the very thing that represents their own freedom. There are floor mats and there are flags. The difference should be clear.

My flag is flying in my yard. I have two others folded neatly and put away. I have seen our flag flying in places where the cost was very high. To minimize its significance by any other use beside what it was intended to be is something every citizen should know. Consider the saga of Elian Gonzalez has come to an end. With his return to Cuba goes several millions of dollars in expenses to keep him and his family here in America. I cannot blame anyone, regardless of where they come from, for wanting to come to this country where they can be free. We live in a country where we can travel the length and breadth of it without anyone interfering with our movement.

One thing I have always thought I would like to do is get inside a veteran's mind and analyze his or her thoughts. I have dug deep into the recesses of my own mind but there is nothing with which to compare my thoughts to those of another veteran. We veterans of the Great War are forgotten as individuals, or kept in the back of the mind. We look at today's events, at times, with disgust. But at other times we will travel with our children to school activities or ballgames and see the great number of our youth thriving, having fun, and it restores our faith in human nature. We came home from the war, participated in our communities, started voting and attending school functions, and working at whatever our skills allowed. For the most part we veterans never asked for much, just a chance to pick up our lives, dust away the rigors of war, and forget the part of life we missed while we dealt with the evil forces seeking to destroy our way of life.

11

Fall

"THE SUMMER IS PAST AND we are not all saved." Those words were jotted in a little journal kept by my father. As I write this we commemorate Labor Day, and the labor force that built this country and protected it for over two centuries. I am tempted to pen a letter to my Uncle Sam, the man who pointed to our generation and said, "I Want You!" and we responded. We answered his call and went wherever he told us to go. But now, Uncle Sam, I have a request: I would like to have our country back. When you deemed it necessary you called on us and we carried the battle to far-flung isles, unknown to any of us. We traversed the mountain ranges of Europe and the island chains of the South Pacific, defied the might of Nippon and sent our enemies to meet their end.

Now, throughout our country much real estate is foreign-owned and many thriving businesses ship their profits overseas. Our consumer products are all made in foreign lands and too many are substandard, basically useless to our everyday needs. Stores carry all sorts of religious material such as praying hands and Christmas products made in nations who do not believe in God. Uncle Sam, why did you allow this to happen? Why did you not get a handle on all this before it got out of hand? Our borders are so porous anyone who wants can enter the U.S. with little trouble. We send our children to schools that are understaffed and in disrepair. Our school teachers, to whom we entrust our dear children and grandchildren, are underpaid when they should be the best paid of all professions. After all, where did our engineers start, where did our doctors start? They all started in with a dedicated teacher patiently teaching them their alphabet. Whatever it takes, Uncle Sam, bring back our manufacturing jobs. Get our own people to adjust their prices and take pride in their products and their employees will take pride in producing something labeled Made in America.

Fall can never come without a reminder of my days on the family farm, when the food we would gather would be all we would have to sustain us through the long winter. September mornings on a hillside farm are cool. The corn is ready for cutting. Dried-up potato vines signal the potatoes are waiting to be dug up and holed up for winter. In my mind I see my father out in the wheat field with his cradle. I see him sweeping up several tines of hay, frequently pausing to wipe the sweat from his furrowed brow. He reaches into the hind pocket of his bib overalls and brings out a long whetstone and stands his scythe up on its end, sharpening the blade for further cutting. September's sun will dry the hay for storing in the barn for the cow and mare. As the trees begin to lose their green, I know that before long it will be cold.

We are past the tender green of spring, the darker green of summer and early fall, and only the most rugged trees retain their beautiful colors. They seem to remain as the rear guard, to watch for the ravages of the coming storms of winter. They are sentinels, ever watchful, ever aware that their time of tumbling down is near. When their leaves fall it will be time to put away their beauty until next year.

And I sit here now counting my blessings at having seen so many of these beautiful displays of nature which man can never duplicate. I know according to nature's way that the time of my departure is near. Soon I will go and join my family and beloved wife; soon there will be only these words. I want to make them words of encouragement, not of dismay or anger. Words to live by, to worship with and most of all to record the great love I have for all. As I once wrote of my nephew Russell, "He has gone on before to mark the trees." So many of those closest to me have gone on to form a welcoming committee. Family, the basic foundation of all we do with our lives.

Another Thanksgiving comes around. But isn't every day one of thanksgiving, especially to those of our generation, our age? I see all the children, grandchildren and great-grandchildren gathered in our home and know it is a blessing most of the world can never experience. A little later today we will gather again at church and celebrate my birthday, a bit early because today all the family is present. What a great blessing on the occasion of my 88th birthday. Great grandson Justin asked to interview me about life during the Great Depression and the Roaring Twenties, when I was a boy. A young man named Cody also came one evening with his video camera to interview me about coal mining in the "old days." In both talks I tried my best to paint a picture they could relate to about both subjects. Had talked to them sooner I would have advised them to read about those eras in my books, *War and Work* and *Coal Bloom*. It is encouraging to see young people wonder about those times, before the modern era which presents so many challenges my generation cannot cope with (any more than today's youth could cope with what we had to face in our youth).

As Mother Nature recedes the sorry condition of many of our hillsides in West Virginia is again revealed. For a time She could hide the throw-away cartons, cans, milk jugs, appliances. Then the harsh winds of winter come and it will be sad to see. It is not a welcome sight for those coming home for the holidays to see abandoned cars, stoves, tires and so on dotting the hillsides. The saddest part is that it is us who do it. I use the word "us" in a general sense, for it really is not everyone. But there are many who simply do not care, and that in itself is sad. The litter law has no teeth and as we travel our state roads there are not even very many signs saying "Do not litter." Sometimes the mere presence of these signs is enough to make one stop and think. But children can be trained not to litter. That's the bottom line, and where care for the environment has to start.

12

Winter

Early winter brings another election. With a presidential campaign well under way as I write this, it will be interesting to see what percentage of registered voters actually turn out to vote. Historically it has been very low. It makes us realize that we are all living our lives based on the will of a minority of citizens. This applies to all elections, whether city, county, state, primary, or general. Even when a decision affects everyone in the country, the minority decides. This generally applies to our churches, schools, union halls, parent-teacher meetings, and many other community functions.

Everyone should be involved in decision-making such as this. It is painful to watch people who live in other countries put forth the efforts they do to just vote. They may walk two or three days and stand in line another day to exercise the right we take so lightly. Undoubtedly it is the inherent right of all Americans to vote or not; this is, after all, a democracy, and no one is punished for not casting his or her ballot. Consider the election in pre-invasion

Iraq. Only one person ran for the office of president. In our country we are not told what or whom to vote for, and we have all the time we need to figure it out. We just need more people to participate so we know that a majority has spoken.

The dark green of late summer and the blaze of fall color haven't been gone long, but as I pulled out of my driveway I saw the snow line very plainly on the mountain. As I ascended the mountain I saw that every little twig was encased in ice and snow. Everything was pure and white and as I gazed at the mountain slopes I saw the cutaway logging roads zigzagging across the face of the hills. On one hillside the power line right of way described a wide white track revealing a long, open valley. It was truly beautiful. I am always amazed at the work of Mother Nature, and when the tender spring sprouts come out I will marvel at their appearance too.

A snowy and wintery day, as it has been snowing for two days. Not much accumulation but very cold. The temperature is hanging just below freezing, which started me thinking about a few things relative to getting old. There were many days in my own life when I would look at people, those my age and either older or a bit younger, and try to figure out what they were thinking. Do they worry? Are they thinking their days are about ended? Are they in pain? Obviously the general answer to these questions is, yes. But what about the individual? What is he looking at and what is he thinking? Should he answer the youth? Why not? Someday they too will reach this same age, God permitting, and they will look back through the decades and remember.

Inwardly, I feel just the same as many years ago, although I know I've lost a good bit of movement and tire easily. I feel the small tendrils reaching, searching and attaching onto some of my thoughts. A bit of memory here, a bit of wondering what I was looking for, a feeling of helplessness at losing a face and name. Where do I know that person from? Old folks generally have the grace and wisdom to know they are winding down. But younger people would envy their elders if they only they knew what perspective time has granted them. I wish I could take my experience and somehow tuck it into the minds and bodies of my grandsons. But that is farfetched even to imagine. Leave them alone, let them build their own experiences, and then they will always have them.

Early December can never pass without our nation pausing to remember the great destruction visited upon us on the "day that will live in infamy," December 7. What was it like on the home front on Pearl Harbor day? Just as with the end of the war, as I describe above, I remember very clearly where I was on that fateful day. I was already in the service, a Marine Sergeant home on weekend leave. People were going about their daily activities with no hint of the impending disaster. I was with my future wife, Recie, that morning and was not listening to the radio so we missed the original newscast.

I was enroute to Princeton to catch my ride back to Camp LeJeune, N.C. when I heard the news. The driver turned on the car radio and every station was carrying the news of Pearl Harbor. When we arrived at the Grand Hotel in Princeton they also had their radio on and were announcing all Marines must return to camp immediately.

There were six Marines in our group and we all loaded up in a borrowed 1937 Chevrolet four-door sedan and hit the road. We broke the speed limit in every town we went through. We stopped briefly at a diner in North Carolina and the story covered the entire front page of the newspaper with two-inch print: *War!* We entered the city of Durham doing about 70 miles an hour. We hadn't gone far until a policeman on a motorcycle pulled up alongside. He looked into the car, saw that we were all Marines, and pulled around in front of the car. He motioned us to follow him. He escorted us through the city, siren blowing and lights flashing. The homefront changed that day for all of us, and the interested reader can pick up my own story in my previous books.

January is a cold and forbidding month. I can handle this cold, for in my youth I witnessed many winters for worse than today's. I suppose it is my age that makes it unbearable at times. But we cope with it and take it one day at a time. A strange thought came to me about my own father. I realized that I never quite picture him at any particular time in his life, the reason being the difference in our ages. He was born in our country's first centennial year, 1876, in April, so he was forty-three when I was born on November 26, 1919. This calculation made me realize I did not fully know what he was about during the stages of his life until I reached a certain age. I do know he and my mother endured many hardships during the Depression, but what was he thinking then? I can only place myself in his shoes and imagine what I would have done. Growing up in the twenties and during the Depression of the thirties I can look back now and appreciate him even more. He must have been considering every day how to keep his huge family fed and clothed, and how to advance our meager education.

Only now, as I have passed the age he was when we had to leave our familiar mountain home for the coal camp of Helen, can I begin to really know what he was feeling. I look back on at my own feelings in a given year and think about him at that age. When I feel the pangs of age I can reach back through time and feel his pain also. The question comes to mind: Was I as conscious as I should have been of his condition and responsibility?

The day I went away to war, I know now that the grief of both mom and dad was almost unbearable, but was I thinking of them and what they felt? I see now the youth of our nation defending our country and I ache for their parents. Thank God I never had one of my own go to war. I firmly believe God, in His infinite wisdom, balanced the scales for me and chose not to put me through that ordeal, for He decreed that the responsibility I showed for country and family and home was enough. I rest now in the thought that one day when I stand before Him He will say, "Well done thou good and faithful servant." I pray He will continue to bless us in the meantime.

February began on a cold, snowy morning. The wind chill kept me from any outside activity. It was a time for inside repairs of outside tools, and preparation for the coming planting season. I recall my father working on such tools and imagine how he would have accomplished the job: *The old-timer looks over his assortment of gardening tools. He sees a splintered handle here, a broken one there, and he ponders in his mind what materials he may need. Dry and seasoned hickory or ash. He sharpens his double-bit ax and sets off into the forest in quest of the timber he needs. Finding an adequate supply he returns to his home and begins his work. He uses his sharpened hatchet to rough in the wood to near size. Next he improvises a suitable clamp to hold the rough lumber and seeks out his drawing knife. He sharpens it and begins to shape the material into the handle. He looks around for a broken fruit jar and breaks shards into several small pieces with which to scrape and smooth the wood. When he's done he picks up a choice piece of sandstone and rubs it over his the handle.*

Not every February was as bitter cold as this one. I recall the first house we lived in in Helen, in "Pig Pen Bottom" as it was called. I recall working outside on my front porch one February night, repairing our steps, with sweat roiling down my face and t-shirt and bugs flying around the porch light.

But this February found me doing what my Father did, working inside the house and only going out in the workshop when the temperature rose above freezing. Sometimes the weather forced us inside for ten days or more. The winter really came to us hard and fast with very cold temperatures. It is easy to find something to keep busy with on cold wintery days. Much of the time I stayed near Recie to keep her company. I remember Valentine's Day with Recie and the many heart-shaped boxes of candy I purchased for her. We still have one of those big boxes, where we keep all her graduation cards.

As a winter storm approached, bringing ice, snow, and frozen rain, I could not help but think back to my teens and the progress the nation, and world, have made in forecasting weather conditions. We were warned of this coming storm, so people could go out to the grocery store and stock up on staples to last a few days. But as I grew up we had no television, radio or any other way of knowing what was coming; we would just wake up one morning and see the ice clinging to the trees and snow covering the ground. My brother, Buck, and I would take advantage of storms like this. After breakfast we'd take off into the woods and up the mountain with a saw and axe. It was a perfect time to cut down any dead trees (and sometimes a huge live one) and trim all the limbs off and give it a shove downhill. We would pause for a few minutes listening for it to hit the creek below. Sometimes we would have three or four sticking up out of Cedar Creek. This provided an ample supply of firewood, with which we heated our home and cooked our meals.

The month wears on and brings memories of past snows. I remember seasons opposite to ours in Australia, the "land down under," where the Southern Cross dominates the sky and everything rotates just the opposite from our North Star. A friend from the south was amazed, being accustomed to only green. The changes in the mountain colors contrast vividly in my mind with the lush jungles of the South Pacific, during our October offenses on Guadalcanal and the assaults at the Matanikau River, where the Japanese tanks and troops came and were repelled on three separate fronts. I spent two winters in the South Pacific, serving there December, 1942 through June of 1944 and sometimes my memories get tangled up. I see total green on one front with jungle growth, and on the other I see West Virginia's earth colors mingling with the permanent green of the pine trees. Hardy mountain oak and hickory leaves cling longer than most others, as if in defiance of a mother's call to the earth. My bare feet kick up leaves into the wind. Chestnut trees drop their bounty and falling leaves cover the chestnuts over and preserve them from bitter winter blasts, while in the jungle the monsoon comes and driving, relentless rain pours down as if from buckets. There is no place to hide from the onslaught of Mother Nature's force and we ride out the storm, just as we know the enemy must be doing. In my mind I hear the ringing of the cow bells on distant hills and see trails lead off to where they graze. Here and there a blaze of red, as wild plants show off their berries. The animal trails show signs of recent passage but they do not bother me in the least. This is their home.

In *War and Work* I briefly mentioned my time in Guantanamo, Cuba, which is in the news frequently these days. Little did I know then, as I embarked for Cuba on December 23, 1940, that the small base where I was stationed would become notorious as a prison for accused terrorists. As I stated in *War and Work*, Cuba was hard duty. There was literally no base when we landed. We carved our tent camp from the burning landscape of the desert. We broke rock and mixed and poured cement for the mess hall base and all the other buildings. While the building of "Gitmo" continued, I walked guard duty with a fully loaded .03 and full ammo belt. After this initial work we began intensive training in the art of jungle warfare and the art of boat landings. These were in preparation for the days to come in actual combat in the South Pacific. The training in Cuba hardened us for our place in history, which would mark our division among the famous in the history of American warfare.

Liberty in Gitmo was a joke. There were no cities close by so liberty was on another nearby island, which required riding on a bus, a train and a boat. The whole trip took

Practicing for the South Pacific. U.S. Marine Corps archives.

about fifteen hours one way, and twenty-four hours was the limit for liberty. By the time we made the trip it was time to return to base. There was no time for enjoyment, so most of us just briefly sampled the spirits of the place and headed back.

Christmas in Cuba lost its true meaning for us, in that those of us from the hills could never associate Christmas with sandy beaches and cactus. When we left Gitmo we left a place for future recruits to train for whatever their futures held. But in our few months in Cuba we also built our unit into what our country needed. We had been parched by the intense heat, taught to survive, perfected amphibious landings, and been hardened into a lean fighting machine. When U.S. commanders began to look for a unit ready for battle in the South Pacific, the answer came immediately: "The First Marine Division is the only military unit combat-ready."

Our brief stint in Portsmouth Navy Yard proved a source of friction between the base Navy men, dressed in their crisp blues, and the brown, not-so-well-dressed fleet marines; the latter set a bad example according to the base commander. "Get these fleet marines the hell out of here!"

So, the raggedy-assed marines were again on the march. But our time had not yet come.

We arrived at our base in New River and saw that our tent city had saplings growing up through the floors, and we knew they had finally found a place to put this lean bunch out of humanity's reach. So, except for our brief stay in Australia, "the Old Breed" never really came out of the boondocks until we stepped off the ship in San Diego, after our battles were done.

So the months of December, 1940 through June, 1944 are welded together into one long chain of memory. They remain in my mind as if all that occurred between those dates happened just yesterday.

As I write this, my last few nights have been filled with dreams. One or two were connected to the long-ago wars of my youth. Some recalled my mining years, others still different facets of life. I suppose these dreams are triggered by ongoing worry, or the plain fatigue of age. Word came just a couple of days ago of the demise of my old and dear friend Lt. Colonel A. L. "Scoop" Adams. I am more and more reminded of the title of a TV program I saw years ago, John Nesbitt's Passing Parade. It would appear that each of us who were participants of World War II has his own "passing parade" and I can name so many who have gone on before me. M. O. Darsey, Andrelio, Kelly, and many others. We World War II veterans are leaving here at the rate of more than twelve hundred per day. Soon the responsibility for this country will fall fully on the generation we spawned, commonly called Baby Boomers. We were referred to as The Greatest Generation by one learned newsman, and truly our generation was called on to do the impossible with the unavailable, to go to the unknown and perform tasks never before asked of a people. But we answered the call, we went, we conquered, we came home and rebuilt a nation, and contributed to rebuilding a world. Now we leave it in the hands of our youth. Are you ready? Are you willing?

Today I think of another "day that will live in infamy," September 11, 2001. Flags fly at half mast and families of the many dead from both occasions remember the days tearfully. Both anniversaries mark the invasion of our country. On December 7 the harbingers of death left a return address. The second attack was covert. They came in seeming innocence and with no obvious goal in mind, all the while plotting to bring death and mayhem to New York City. Now these evil forces have, under the name of their god, declared a holy war against our nation and way of life. They too must be held accountable. But the methods our leaders have so far chosen to take the fight to them have caused festering discontent and division among our people.

Our nation was built by those who came here in search of a better way of life, but many of those coming now come the wrong way. They do not pass through Ellis Island with proper papers, where so many knelt to kiss the soil of freedom. Instead, thousands sneak across our porous borders.

After Christmas comes a new year. Every January my thoughts drift back to January, 1944, when I was still fighting in the South Pacific, this time on New Britain. Visions of Tully's ring, Newcomb's knee, and Dykstra's crooked elbow—all described at length in my previous books—mingle with the stench of the jungle rot. I carry plenty of physical reminders of my time in the South

Pacific jungles. For example, my fingernails still routinely come off because of an incurable fungus, just as they did those many years ago on Guadalcanal. After trying many remedies over the years I have concluded I will just have to live with this painful condition.

New Britain was a hard taskmaster, but we could still laugh. I remember once we were back behind the lines for regrouping, resupplying and relaxing, but there was still all the dangers of the jungle and the Japanese, so we were required to wear or carry a weapon at all times, even to chow. I had "acquired" a Japanese flag and one Marine struck up a trade with me, the flag for a forty-five automatic service pistol. A bit later another approached me with a trade in mind, this time for a thirty-eight special revolver with a belt and cutaway holster. I traded with him and consequently when chow time came I carried the revolver. Because it was so hot in the jungle we wore only our skivvies around the camp and would twist the bottoms and roll them up until they looked like modern day bikinis. Imagine me going to chow with a pith helmet and skivvies, the thirty-eight slung around my hip on a forty-five degree angle, low slung, ready for the draw! Of course, I looked as good as the others.

13

Recie

IN THE FALL OF 2005 we were vacationing in Delaware with daughter Gloria and her husband Ralph. It was to be the last vacation for Recie and me. Shortly thereafter her health began to decline and it seemed she grew progressively worse by the day. In addition to many other problems, tests showed that she was not getting enough oxygen to her organs, so she was forced to use an oxygen machine part of each day. She hated being tethered to it. She began to get more confused and disoriented and didn't sleep well. Then our family doctor sent her to a clinic in Princeton for a bladder scan, as her kidneys had not been active for over a week. The young lady who was supposed to do the scan could not perform the procedure with Recie in such a state. She asked the doctor what to do about it. He simply said, "Send her home."

Fateful words.

Instead of admitting her to the hospital and giving her some relief this forced her to ride sixty miles home and then, after again consulting our family doctor, another twenty miles to the hospital in Beckley. In the emergency room they extracted 1100 cc of urine from her bladder and found that she had developed a urinary tract infection. Her decline steepened. She was kept in the hospital as long as our insurance would permit. The UTI continued to plague her, not responding to progressively stronger drugs, until finally it was necessary to insert a catheter, which lowered her already low morale even further.

She went through a succession of visits with home care therapists and nurses but none of it was of much help. Her blood count stayed very low and with all the infection that had invaded her body she fell further into a deep depression, on top of her preexisting neuritis and other conditions. We wondered how things could get worse.

In mid-December of 2005 she was hospitalized again, and her slow decline into depression took a new turn, plunging her deeper and deeper into depths known only to her Maker. Whatever the cause, she began to have strange visions in the daytime and vivid and terrifying dreams at night. She would dream of dying and going to hell, which in turn prompted her to make everyone leave the room—especially me—for fear we would be swept into hell with her. It brought to mind Psalms 139: "O Lord, thou hast searched me and know me. Search me, O Lord, and know my heart, try me and know my thoughts and see if there be any wicked way in me and lead me in the way of everlasting." The psalm says wherever we go He will be there with us. Even as these dreams invaded her thoughts I feel the Lord never left her side.

In the waning days of 2005 sickness invaded both of us and we were in dire straits. Recie would not sleep, and would permit no light at all in the room. Even a small reading light bothered her to the extent that I quit my lifelong habit of reading at bedtime. Many times as we slept together a noise would awaken me and I would find her kneeling beside her oxygen machine, determined that it was not functioning properly. Both of us became sleep-deprived and worn down physically.

But it was very difficult to know what to do. Recie would call Gloria at all hours of the night just to talk to her. Gloria was able, with tender love of a daughter, to calm her to some extent. Recie would also call her sister Stevie and her husband Harry very early in the morning, sometimes at three a.m., and they would very kindly come up and look at her oxygen machine to reassure her. I would be awakened shortly and troubleshoot the thing myself to demonstrate to her that it was working properly, but to no avail. She was obsessed that it was harmful to her.

As January of 2006 came it became painfully obvious we were no longer able to care for ourselves. At the insistence of Gloria and our granddaughter Jackie we moved in with Gloria and Ralph near Mt. Hope. But Recie's condition continued to decline. Gloria moved her king-size bed into storage and set up a smaller bed for Recie in her bedroom. The oxygen machine continued to be a mystery to Recie, keeping her in a state of agitation. She would awaken at all hours of the night and slip out of bed. Gloria would find her down in front of the machine with a small flashlight trying to read whatever was printed on it.

Finally we moved the machine into the bedroom where I slept. But Recie would simply get out of bed, follow the air hose, and again try to decipher the instructions on the machine. During the day I put enough hose on the machine to allow her to come all the way into the dining room, but she would come only to the doorway and stop. No amount of persuasion would prompt her to come and sit down. She kept insisting she was not working in order to pay her way in the house, as she put it, implying that she had been chained up without enough chain to come to the table. The oxygen hose had become figurative chains of bondage to her, keeping her confined, in her mind, to only the length of the hose.

We made the difficult decision that we couldn't continue to live in Helen, our home for almost fifty years. It was just too far to town, over Tams Mountain, and the house had too many stairs. We determined to build a small new house across the little stream on Ralph and Gloria's back property and on January 23, 2006, work began. House plans were selected, a roadway was laid down, and contractors began laying the foundation.

Recie was hospitalized several times again in February and her condition seemed to worsen each time. Our doctors said she needed therapy and so we arranged for her to enter a rehabilitation center, Heartland of Beckley, on the first day of March. She had already had pneumonia and now she could not swallow properly—her food would go down into her lungs instead of her stomach. In the rehab center she began intensive therapy for her speech, walking, and swallowing. They worked with her diligently, and she gave it everything she had, but with no success. All attempts to restore her neck

Recie and I, 1940's.

muscles in order for her to swallow were fruitless. We were forced to agree to have a feeding tube installed, so she would not starve. We hoped this was a temporary measure.

After almost two months we brought her home, again in worse shape than when she went in. She had suffered a fall at Heartland and hit her lower back on a piece of furniture, which developed very quickly into a terrible bed sore. At first it seemed impossible we could keep this from killing her, as bedsores do so many older people, but under the watchful eye of Gloria and a host of folks from the Hospice Foundation, ExtendaCare, and home caregivers, we cared for that wound every day for almost two years—the rest of her life—reducing it eventually from tennis ball size to no larger than a pencil eraser.

We brought her back from Heartland to Gloria's house the last week in April. Meanwhile, our new house was taking shape nicely and the work continued quickly. We watched its progress from Gloria's porch. Ralph and I did a great deal of the work ourselves. Members of their church also pitched in with every kind of help imaginable. While our new house was being built my prayer every morning and night always ended the same way, with my asking the Lord to let Recie live long enough to spend at least a little time with me in our new home. Without her presence, it would never be home for me.

But Recie had to be admitted to the hospital on a regular basis, and each stay seemed to make her worse. She would come home weaker than when she went in, and she usually picked up a MRSA infection. She developed an allergy to the main anti-MRSA drug, so had to go on longer and longer doses of less effective medicines.

But the Lord answered my prayer. The first of week of June, 2006, we moved into our new house. Our feeling of security improved greatly knowing our daughter and son in law were near to take care of us as our own ability failed.

July found Recie again in the hospital for a ten day stay, and another in August. More infection and a gradual ebbing strength.

As a family we made a difficult decision: No more hospitals. From the fall of 2006 she had home care from whatever source Gloria could recruit. (Gloria is a master manager of such things.) I could have never have cared for Recie on my own, and am so grateful to her and everyone who gave of their time and energy.

Fall rolled on. Recie seemed to stabilize somewhat. She did not have so many frightening dreams and visions, but she was very weak.

We settled into something like a normal routine. I began building a small workshop adjacent to the new house. On Thanksgiving Day I sat down to catalog all the things I had to be thankful for. We had a new home, new friends, and really a good neighborhood in which to spend our remaining days. And Recie had been able to come live with me.

Family has always been central to our lives. Coming home from the war in 1945, back to hometown and family, made me realize that I wanted to make up for lost time. I had just been married shortly after twenty-eight months in the South Pacific. Recie and I began to think more and more about family unity, and we began the Christmas tradition of having both our families together for dinner. We have continued this since 1948. We host our own family, our children, grandchildren and two great-grandchildren, plus any sisters and brothers and friends who happen to be around. We gather at Easter, Thanksgiving, Christmas Eve and at a family reunion each summer.

So it was very joyous, despite Recie's condition, that our entire family was able to join us for Thanksgiving 2006— all our children, grandchildren, and great-grandchildren, not to mention many other relatives and in-laws. I sat in amazement as pictures and video were taken. Laughter echoed throughout the house. Footprints and fingerprints began to give our new house the memories to make it our home. I thought, oh God, how great thou art!

November passed and we celebrated my birthday, then Recie's in December. We blew out the candles and when the smoke cleared it brought Recie to age eighty-four and me to eighty-seven. I knew that we had been blessed with many "dividend" years beyond the biblical three score and ten.

Winter was held at bay by unseasonably warm southern winds until the middle of January, when the jet stream moved east and encased us in cold arctic air. It was too cold to work in my shop so I passed the time writing and repairing small items inside.

Attendants came and went, caring for Recie in her long struggle. All seemed to grow to love her, because that's the kind of woman she was. She had the ability to get into people's hearts and touch them, to understand their troubles and, even from her sick bed, give them a comforting thought. Recie could do little more than lie and watch television and talk a little but she and I still laughed together, still wept together, and had many moments of happiness even during her final days. New friends, a new house and a new beginning in different environs, but even in difficult circumstances we were content.

Recie continued to surprise us all. Her physicians held out little hope she would survive 2006, but she slowly gained strength and was able to walk from her bedside around the room several times a day, leaning on a caretaker.

February wound down, and despite our previous vow we agreed to admit Recie to the hospital once more, this time for a blood transfusion. This gave her a little extra energy and strength. Her doctors had nearly given up on her a year before, but now she was putting up a fight like the Marine wife she was. Late February saw some improvement in her overall health, as the huge bedsore contracted at Heartland was healing nicely. She had been through many changes during the last year, preoccupied as she was with thoughts of hell, the sky chasing her, and forgetting her family for a time. We had all scribbled many notes and left them by her bedside so she could read who she was, who I was, and who were her children and grandchildren. Now her mind was clearer and though she was still weak she recognized her loved ones and could converse with them.

Recie remained with us throughout another cycle of seasons, her bedsore nearly healed, walking short distances her own with just a little support. As her mind began to clear she returned more to her old self and kept us laughing, her wit sometimes directed at me and sometimes at others. Gloria's husband Ralph was indispensable. He had lost his own mother as a teenager and treated Recie with the utmost tenderness. One day she looked up at Ralph and out of the blue said, "Ralph, I love you." That was very special for him. Sometimes he joked with her and she with him. She would tell us both to be quiet but when I joked with her she looked up at me with a beautiful little smile. She said, "You're crazy, Thurman." I told her, I know, but it helps in this old world.

With Recie at one of the many Marine Corps reunions we were privileged to attend.

For the Fourth of July Gloria had a cookout and Recie agreed to go for the first time in two years. She put on a pair of slacks and we helped her across the yard to Ralph and Gloria's driveway. She visited with all of us and then wanted to go back over to our house. Our home. We were all so proud of her and praised her effort. We hoped to get her up walking more and begin working towards removing her various tubes.

With her bedsore almost healed, Recie's pain decreased. She still could not eat, being fed entirely by a feeding tube. She would dream and then question me about such things as beef roast and stewed apples. She remembered when

I would fry oysters every Saturday night for her and our neighbor Ann. Recie told me she remembered they had been browned exactly right.

Our plan was to begin our own home physical therapy and try to get Recie to talking more loudly, maybe begin to eat a little by mouth, for the pleasure of eating if not for the nutrition. Our goal was to restore her quality of life as far as possible. Having nearly given up hope, we began to gain some back.

Recie hung in there through the dog days of August, still giving us her beautiful little smile occasionally. Our day to day ritual changed little for many months. Her primary caregiver, Pam, came at nine a.m. and stayed until about five, when Gloria and took over. A different caregiver came on Saturday and Sunday. We had no choice but to take things as they came.

Autumn days can pass with uncanny rapidity. They come, they go, and every day in this period seemed the same in many ways. I would get up anywhere from three a.m. to seven a.m. and begin my day with some writing, paying some bills, and reading, until I heard Recie call for me. From that first call until the caregiver came I took care of Recie's medications and fed her. She would talk a little and then fall into a deep slumber. I would go about the house until she called again. Usually

With Recie, 2001.

she just wanted to talk. Sometimes she would ask about her pocketbook or cooking utensils and I knew in her dreams she was preparing to go out or to cook dinner for the family. But when she was awake she knew what was going on at all times and often when we thought she was asleep we would hear from her if she disagreed with something she heard. That in itself gave us much pleasure, to know she was still with us.

The days grew short and the nights grew longer. In late October we had great news: The doctor caring for her wound told us that Recie's bedsore had healed to the extent that we could cease using the Woundvac, so she would be connected to one less piece of machinery.

The Saturday after Thanksgiving all the family gathered at church to give Recie an early birthday party. It was a great occasion, with refreshments, a birthday cake with her picture on it, and a poster board with many photos of her life, from her beautiful youth to her graceful eightieth year. Speeches were called for and I led off. I started with, "A funny thing happened to me on my way to eighty." I told about moving to Helen and described an anniversary gift I gave Recie when work was slow and my paydays irregular. I came in from work and set a commode lid and a gallon of paint on the table. I told Recie, "Happy anniversary!" Everyone laughed. In all the days of our married life, all our anniversaries were special, but our gift of love on any given day was enough.

My prayers had been answered far beyond what I had any right to ask or hope for. Recie had been able to come live with me in our new home for twenty months. But the first two weeks of January found her weakening to a point from which I knew she would not return. On January 15, as I sat with her, Gloria on one side and me on the other, she passed from this life. I read the Twenty-third psalm and talked gently to her as her breath began to get shallow. I reassured her that I would go with her and row her across the river in a shiny boat with golden oars, then I would have to return to this vale of tears to await the time I would join her.

Christmas may recall the humid the South Pacific or a bitter cold winter on the family farm. August brings to mind Guadalcanal or a sweltering Cedar Creek. January will always be the month I parted with my precious Recie.

As I write this, it's been several months since her passing, days of personal grief and memories of days gone by. It seems such a short time ago when Recie and I sat as youthful lovers and talked about life and time, always ending on a note of hope for the future. My sixty-two years with her showed me facets of her character a casual observer might miss. I learned there were moments when she would rather be alone, but most of the time she loved to laugh and have a good time with her children and grandchildren. She dearly loved all of them, and always sought to see to their needs. She made many friends as she passed through this life. She would never speak evil of anyone and if one of us spoke harshly about someone she would tell us if we couldn't say something good about a person, don't say anything. She lived by these principles and tried to instill the same kindness in those around her.

She carried me through many dark days when I would have given up. She called upon her inner strength and found the words to calm a troubled soul. She was everything a man could desire in a mate. I miss her so very much but know she is in a place where there is no pain.

We struggle daily without her and I suppose that will be true as long as I live, but I told her in the last moments of life, as I symbolically rowed her across the river, not to go very far out but to pick out a good soft cloud and wait for me. I know it will not be long until I see her. There is no way of knowing when, but doesn't the scripture say life is as a vapor?

God granted us the future I could only dream of as I prepared to die for my country on a far away island, and toiled daily in the depths of the earth mining coal. He gave us three wonderful children and they in turn endowed us with many grandchildren and great-grandchildren. I thank God each night and morning for what He gave to us. He not only provided for our needs but greatly surpassed what is needed to sustain life. Working in unity with each other provided a healthy and wonderful life for Recie and me, and we always walked it together. I insisted from the very start of our wedded life that she walk beside me, not in front or behind. Knowing she was there beside me in spirit, even when I was at work, helped me through many difficult times, for I knew at day's end I would return to her love and devotion and all my wonderful children and grandchildren. I fought a good fight with war and sickness and disease and hard toil and it was only with Recie's help that I survived. She abides forever in my memory.

The End

Appendix

The following originally appeared in Lexington Family *magazine.*

Bound by a Book
By David Miller

"I've known your father for more than half a century, starting when our platoon was formed at Parris Island," the letter began. The writer, "Scoop" Adams, was my father's commanding officer in K Company, First Marine Division, in World War II.

He described their experience in boot camp, their training in Cuba, and finally their landing on the island of Guadalcanal, where the U.S. began its first counteroffensive on Japanese-held soil.

"The night before the landing we were told not to expect to survive," he wrote. "In fact, most of us didn't." Within a few weeks seven of every 10 men in their company were dead or wounded in some of the most ruthless fighting of the war, or had contracted any of several debilitating tropical diseases.

The company spent four torturous months on the island, nearly starving as the Japanese cut off their supply lines. But in the end they took and held the island and secured America a crucial foothold in the South Pacific. My father went on to fight in several other historic battles in the Solomon Islands.

I knew that much of the public story. But the details were new to me: the new-model rifles they were issued, with wooden stocks that swelled to uselessness in the moist tropics; scrabbling for any type of food, including wormy rice; the taste of coffee grounds brewed eight times, with leaves and mud mixed in.

My father, a "gunny" sergeant and drill instructor, was lucky to have survived these battles. Like many of the other survivors he faced a hard time back home. He developed malaria, despite faithfully taking Atabrine, and because of the disease for years he could eat little but skim milk, oatmeal and toast. His toenails and fingernails fell off as the result of an untreatable fungus infection. He startled awake many nights, haunted by the faces of the men he killed, or his buddies who were killed.

We would now call his condition post-traumatic stress syndrome, made worse by a difficult job in the West Virginia coal mines, the only place he could find work after the war. On top of all these came responsibility for a growing family.

Yet while I was growing up I knew my father as a gentle, kind man, very funny, always willing to fix a neighbor kid's bike, always lending a hand. He never turned to alcohol as many did, and rarely spoke harshly to his family, although

I saw occasional flashes of a deep inner anger. And when as a teenager I became good friends with a Japanese boy, my father welcomed him like a member of the family.

As I've gotten older I've wondered, How does a man change himself from killer to father? From expecting to die to appreciating each day?

As a boy I knew the outlines of his life, that he had grown up in Depression-era Appalachia, barefoot, no electricity, hardly enough food for a large flock of brothers and sisters; that he served in the war; and that he worked in the mines. Beyond that I knew little.

From time to time over the years I talked to him about his experiences, and although he patiently answered my questions the details never seemed to add up to a complete picture of the man.

But I knew that from time to time he had been able to put down in writing things he could never say directly to another human being. Never academically trained—it was a struggle in the coal fields just to finish high school—he nevertheless made it a lifelong habit to sit at his battered Royal manual typewriter and bang out a few pages now and then about whatever was on his mind, including war memories, short stories, poems, songs, and family lore. Except for a few letters to the editor he filed everything away in a big black binder, and few people go to see it.

I asked several times whether he'd like to publish these memoirs as a bona fide book and he always refused, saying he wrote for himself and never intended strangers to read it. In truth, much of what he wrote was painfully tender and revealing, although even the darkest pieces have some humorous element. Two years ago on his 80th birthday, after we chatted about our children, his grandchildren, and his generation's legacy, something changed. He agreed to publish it—if I would help him.

With the same can-do spirit he brought to everything else, my father mastered e-mail, and for months we exchanged messages almost daily, as I asked him to clarify a point or add some detail or identify a person in one of the many photographs we scanned and exchanged by e-mail. We contacted many of his old friends and incorporated their recollections, taping and transcribing their comments for quoting in the book. Scoop wrote a foreword. Dr. Joanna Roberts, a longtime family friend and highly respected southern West Virginia physician, contributed a glowing introduction. I had many of the short pieces retyped and began piecing them together in chronological order.

After six months we had 250 solid pages. The book broke naturally into three parts: his poor but relatively happy boyhood in the mountains; a long middle section covering the war years; and a final third describing three decades of life as a coal miner.

Only then did I begin to see my father in full. Sifting through the material again and again made me realize that the values he'd adopted as a young man—singing to the mountains as he drove the family's few cattle home, sheltering barefoot in a hollow tree as a summer thunderstorm passed—nurtured him through the dark days that followed. Living off the land prepared him for the hellish South Pacific better than any urban upbringing could have, and probably saved his life. Attending the slaughter of farm animals gave him respect for the cycle of birth and death and rebirth, providing him hope for spiritual resurrection after the horrors of Guadalcanal and the long, slow struggle up from the darkness of the mines.

Every family has its own mythology connecting it to larger, even historic forces. Neither my father nor I knew until we started researching the book that his great-great-grandfather was the first postmaster and schoolteacher in what was then the most rural part of southwestern Virginia. I like to believe that his regard for education has been expressed in my own father's habit of reading and writing, and that a natural love of learning will flower in my own children. I want them to understand how my father's life rolled forward from the sunny pre-strip mining hills of West Virginia through the figurative darkness of World War II and the literal darkness of the mines. I want them to see that his very survival was made possible by the belief that he was fighting for a future in which the most degraded man could rebuild himself as a steady, honest worker, a faithful husband, a patient father.

I want them to believe that like their grandfather they are bred in the bone with the strength to meet their own challenges, large or small, with courage, generosity of spirit, and especially a sense of humor. His life demonstrates that not only is that one way to live, it's the only way.

The author is the father of Molly and Andrew.

The Guadalcanal Campaign: A Summary

Adapted from Wikipedia, the free encyclopedia, www. wikipedia.org, and reprinted pursuant to the GNU Free Documentation License.

Major features of Guadalcanal. U.S. Marine Corps archives.

Date	
August 7, 1942 – February 9, 1943	

Location	Commanders	
Guadalcanal in the Solomon Islands	Robert Ghormley	Harukichi Hyakutake
	William Halsey, Jr.	Isoroku Yamamoto
Result	Alexander Vandegrift	Nishizo Tsukahara
Allied strategic victory	Alexander Patch	Jinichi Kusaka
	Richmond K. Turner	Hitoshi Imamura

Belligerents		Strength	
Allied forces:	Empire of Japan	60,000 (ground forces)[4]	36,200 (ground forces)[5]
United States		**Casualties and losses**	
		1,768 dead (ground),	24,600–25,600 dead (ground),
Australia		4,911 dead (naval),	3,543 dead (naval),
		420 dead (aircrew),	1,200 dead (aircrew),
New Zealand		4 captured,	1,000 captured,
		29 ships sunk,	38 ships sunk,
British Empire [1]		615 aircraft destroyed[6]	683–880 aircraft destroyed[7]
Tonga[2]			
Fiji[3]			

The Guadalcanal campaign, also known as the Battle of Guadalcanal, was fought between August 7, 1942, and February 7, 1943, in the Pacific theatre of World War II. This campaign, fought on the ground, at sea, and in the air, pitted Allied forces against Imperial Japanese forces, and was a decisive, strategically significant campaign of World War II. The fighting took place on and around the island of Guadalcanal in the southern Solomon Islands and was the first major offensive launched by Allied forces against the Empire of Japan.

On August 7, 1942, Allied forces, predominantly composed of troops from the United States (U.S.), initiated landings on the islands of Guadalcanal, Tulagi, and Florida in the southern Solomons with the objective of denying their use by Japanese forces as bases to threaten supply routes between the U.S., Australia, and New Zealand. The Allies also intended to use Guadalcanal and Tulagi as bases to support a campaign to eventually isolate the major Japanese base at Rabaul on New Britain. The initial Allied landings overwhelmed the outnumbered Japanese defenders, who had occupied the islands in May 1942, and captured Tulagi and Florida as well as an airfield (later named Henderson Field) that was under construction by the Japanese on Guadalcanal. Surprised by the Allied offensive, the Japanese made several attempts between August and November 1942 to retake Henderson Field on Guadalcanal. These attempts resulted in three major land battles, five large naval battles, and continuous, almost daily, aircraft battles, culminating in the decisive Naval Battle of Guadalcanal in early November 1942, in which the last Japanese attempt to land enough troops to capture Henderson Field was defeated. In December 1942, the

Japanese abandoned further efforts to retake Guadalcanal and successfully evacuated their remaining forces from the island by February 7, 1943, leaving the island in Allied hands.

The Guadalcanal campaign marked the first significant strategic combined arms victory by Allied forces over the Japanese in the Pacific theatre. For this reason, the Guadalcanal campaign is often referred to as a "turning point" in the war. The campaign marked the beginning of the transition by the Allies from defensive operations to the strategic offensive while Japan was thereafter forced to cease strategic offensive operations and instead concentrate on strategic defense. Building on their success at Guadalcanal and elsewhere, the Allies continued their campaign against Japan, ultimately culminating in Japan's defeat and the end of World War II.

Background

On December 7, 1941, Japanese forces attacked the U.S. Pacific fleet at Pearl Harbor, Hawaii. The attack crippled much of the US battleship fleet and precipitated a state of war between the two nations. The initial goals of Japanese leaders were to neutralize the U.S. fleet, seize possessions rich in natural resources, and establish strategic military bases to defend Japan's empire in the Pacific and Asia. In further support of these goals, Japanese forces also attacked and took control of the Philippines, Thailand, Malaya, Singapore, the Dutch East Indies, Wake Island, New Britain, and Guam. The US was allied in the war against Japan with other countries including Great Britain, Australia, and New Zealand.[7]

Japanese control of the western Pacific area between May and August 1942. Guadalcanal is located in the lower right center of the map. Two later attempts by the Japanese to extend their defensive perimeter in the south and central Pacific were thwarted in the battles of Coral Sea and Midway. These two strategic victories for the Allies provided them with an opportunity to take the initiative and launch an offensive against the Japanese in the Pacific. [8] The Allies chose the Solomon Islands, specifically the southern Solomon islands of Guadalcanal, Tulagi, and Florida as the location for their first offensive. At this time the Solomon Islands were a protectorate of Great Britain. [9]

Allied strategists knew the Japanese Navy had occupied Tulagi in May 1942 and had constructed a seaplane base near there. Allied concern grew when in early July 1942 the Japanese Navy began constructing a large airfield near Lunga Point on nearby Guadalcanal. By August 1942, the Japanese had about 900 troops on Tulagi and nearby islands, and 2,800 personnel (2,200 of whom were Korean and Japanese construction specialists) on Guadalcanal. These bases, when fully completed, would protect Japan's major base at Rabaul, threaten Allied supply and communication lines, and establish a staging area for possible future offensives against Fiji, New Caledonia, and Samoa. The Japanese planned to deploy 45 fighter and 60 bomber aircraft to Guadalcanal once the airfield was complete.[10]

The Allied plan to attack the Japanese positions in the southern Solomons was conceived by U.S. Admiral Ernest King, Commander in Chief, United States Fleet. He proposed the offensive to deny the use of the southern Solomon islands by the Japanese as bases to threaten the supply routes between the U.S. and Australia, and to use them as starting points for a campaign with the goal of isolating the major Japanese base at Rabaul while also supporting the Allied New Guinea campaign under Douglas MacArthur. The eventual goal was to open the way for the U.S. to retake the Philippines.[11] Admiral Chester Nimitz, Allied commander in chief for Pacific forces, created the South Pacific theater, with Vice Admiral Robert L. Ghormley in command on June 19, 1942, to direct the Allied offensive in the Solomons.[12]

The airfield at Lunga Point on Guadalcanal under construction by Japanese and Korean workers in July 1942. In preparation for the future offensive in the Pacific in May 1942, U.S. Marine Major General Alexander Vandegrift was ordered to move his U.S. 1st Marine Division from the U.S. to New Zealand. Other Allied land, naval, and air force units were sent to establish bases in Fiji, Samoa, New Hebrides, and New Caledonia.[13] Espiritu Santo, New Hebrides, was selected as the headquarters and main base for the southern Solomons offensive, codenamed Operation Watchtower, with the commencement date set for August 7, 1942. At first, the Allied offensive was planned just for Tulagi and the Santa Cruz Islands, omitting Guadalcanal. However, after Allied reconnaissance discovered the Japanese airfield construction efforts on Guadalcanal, its capture was added to the plan, and the Santa Cruz operation was (eventually) dropped.[14]

The Watchtower force, numbering 75 warships and transports (including vessels from both the U.S. and

Australia), assembled near Fiji on July 26, 1942, and engaged in one rehearsal landing prior to leaving for Guadalcanal on July 31.[15] The on-scene commander of the Allied expeditionary force was U.S. Vice Admiral Frank Fletcher. Commanding the amphibious transport force was U.S. Rear Admiral Richmond K. Turner. Vandegrift led the 16,000 Allied (primarily U.S. Marine) infantry involved in the landings.[16]

Landings

Bad weather allowed the Allied expeditionary force to arrive in the vicinity of Guadalcanal unseen by the Japanese on the morning of August 7.[17] The landing force ships split into two groups, with one group assaulting Guadalcanal, and the other Tulagi, Florida, and nearby islands.[18] Allied warships bombarded the invasion beaches while U.S. carrier aircraft bombed Japanese positions on the target islands and destroyed 15 Japanese seaplanes at their base near Tulagi.[19]

Tulagi and two nearby small islands, Gavutu and Tanambogo, were assaulted by 3,000 U.S. Marines on August 7.[20] The 886 Imperial Japanese Navy personnel manning the naval and seaplane bases on the three islands fiercely resisted the Marine attacks.[21] With some difficulty, the U.S. Marines finally secured all three islands; Tulagi on August 8, and Gavutu and Tanambogo by August 9.[22] The Japanese defenders were killed almost to the last man while the Marines suffered 122 killed.[23]

In contrast to Tulagi, Gavutu, and Tanambogo, the landings on Guadalcanal encountered much less resistance. At 09:10 on August 7, Vandegrift and 11,000 U.S. Marines came ashore on Guadalcanal between Koli Point and Lunga Point. Advancing towards Lunga Point, they encountered no resistance except for "tangled" rain forest, and they halted for the night about 1,000 meters from the Lunga Point airfield. The next day, again against little resistance, the Marines advanced all the way to the Lunga River and secured the airfield by 16:00 on August 8. The Japanese naval construction units and naval combat troops, in panic from the warship bombardment and aerial bombing, had abandoned the airfield area and fled about three miles west to the Matanikau River and Point Cruz area, leaving behind food, supplies, intact construction equipment and vehicles, and 13 dead.[24]

During the landing operations on August 7 and August 8, Japanese aircraft based at Rabaul, under the command of Sadayoshi Yamada, attacked the Allied amphibious forces several times, setting afire the U.S. transport George F. Elliot (which sank two days later) and heavily damaging the destroyer USS Jarvis.[25] In the air attacks over the two days, the Japanese lost 36 aircraft, while the U.S. lost 19 aircraft, both in combat and to accident, including 14 carrier fighter aircraft.[26]

After these clashes, Fletcher was concerned about the losses to his carrier fighter aircraft strength, anxious about the threat to his carriers from further Japanese air attacks, and worried about his ship's fuel levels. Without consulting with Vandegrift, Turner, or Ghormley, Fletcher withdrew from the Solomon Islands area with his carrier task forces the evening of August 8 to avoid further losses.[27] As a result of the loss of carrier-based air cover, Turner decided that he would have to withdraw his ships from Guadalcanal, even though less than half of the supplies and heavy equipment on the transport ships needed by the troops ashore had been unloaded.[28] Turner decided, however, to unload as many supplies as possible on Guadalcanal and Tulagi throughout the night of August 8 and then depart with his ships early on August 9.[29]

That night, as the transports unloaded, two groups of Allied warships screening the transports were surprised and defeated by a Japanese force of seven cruisers and one destroyer from the 8th Fleet, based at Rabaul and commanded by Japanese Vice Admiral Gunichi Mikawa. One Australian and three U.S. cruisers were sunk, and one other U.S. cruiser and two destroyers were damaged. The Japanese suffered moderate damage to one cruiser. Mikawa, who was unaware Fletcher had withdrawn with the U.S. carriers, immediately retired to his home bases at Rabaul and Kavieng without attempting to attack the now unprotected Allied transports. Mikawa was concerned about U.S. carrier air attacks during daylight hours if he tarried in the southern Solomons area. Turner withdrew all remaining Allied naval forces by the evening of August 9, leaving the Marines ashore without much of the heavy equipment, provisions, and troops still aboard the transports.[30]

Initial operations

The 11,000 Marines remaining on Guadalcanal initially concentrated on forming a loose defensive perimeter around Lunga Point and the airfield, moving the landed supplies within the perimeter, and finishing the airfield. In four days of intense effort, the supplies were moved from the landing beach into dispersed dumps within the perimeter. Work began on the airfield immediately, mainly using captured Japanese equipment. On August 12, the airfield was named Henderson Field after a Marine aviator killed during the Battle of Midway. By August 18, the airfield was ready for operation.[31] Five days worth of food had been landed from the transports which, along with captured Japanese provisions, gave the Marines a total of 14 days worth of food.[32] To conserve the limited food supplies, the Allied troops were limited to two meals per day.[33] Allied troops encountered a "severe strain" of dysentery soon after the landings, with one in five Marines afflicted by mid-August. Although some of the Korean construction workers surrendered to the Marines, most of the remaining Japanese and Korean personnel gathered just west of the Lunga perimeter on the west bank of the Matanikau River and subsisted mainly on coconuts. A Japanese naval outpost was also located at Taivu Point, about 35 kilometres (22 mi) east of the Lunga perimeter. On August 8, a Japanese destroyer delivered 113 naval reinforcement troops to the Matanikau position.[34]

On the evening of August 12, a 25-man U.S. Marine patrol, led by Lt.Col. Frank Goettge and primarily consisting of intelligence personnel, landed by boat west of the Lunga perimeter, between Point Cruz and the Matanikau River, on a reconnaissance mission with a secondary objective of contacting a group of Japanese troops U.S. forces believed might be willing to surrender. Soon after the patrol landed, a nearby platoon of Japanese naval troops attacked and almost completely wiped out the Marine patrol.[35]

On August 19, Vandegrift sent three companies of the U.S. 5th Marine Regiment to attack the Japanese troop concentration west of the Matanikau. One company attacked across the sandbar at the mouth of the Matanikau river while another crossed the river 1,000 meters inland and attacked the Japanese forces located in Matanikau village. The third landed by boat further west and attacked Kokumbuna village. After briefly occupying the two villages, the three Marine companies returned to the Lunga perimeter, having killed about 65 Japanese soldiers while losing four. This action, sometimes referred to as the "First Battle of the Matanikau", was the first of several major actions around the Matanikau River during the campaign. [36]

On August 20, the escort carrier USS Long Island delivered two squadrons of Marine aircraft to Henderson Field, one of 19 Grumman F4F Wildcats, the other 12 SBD Dauntlesses. The aircraft at Henderson became known as the "Cactus Air Force" (CAF) after the Allied codename for Guadalcanal. The Marine fighters went into action the next day, attacking one of the Japanese bomber air raids that occurred almost daily. On August 22, five U.S. Army P-400 Airacobras and their pilots arrived at Henderson Field.[37]

In response to the Allied landings on Guadalcanal, the Japanese Imperial General Headquarters assigned the Imperial Japanese Army's 17th Army, a corps-sized command based at Rabaul and under the command of Lieutenant General Harukichi Hyakutake, with the task of retaking Guadalcanal from Allied forces. The army was to be supported by Japanese naval units, including the

Combined Fleet under the command of Isoroku Yamamoto which was headquartered at Truk. The 17th Army, at that time heavily involved with the Japanese campaign in New Guinea, had only a few units available to send to the southern Solomons area. Of these units, the 35th Infantry Brigade under Major General Kiyotake Kawaguchi was at Palau, the 4th (Aoba) Infantry Regiment was in the Philippines and the 28th (Ichiki) Infantry Regiment, under the command of Colonel Kiyonao Ichiki, was onboard transport ships near Guam. The different units began to move towards Guadalcanal immediately, but Ichiki's regiment, being the closest, arrived first. A "First Element" of Ichiki's unit, consisting of about 917 soldiers, landed from destroyers at Taivu Point, east of the Lunga perimeter, on August 19.[38]

Underestimating the strength of Allied forces on Guadalcanal, Ichiki's unit conducted a nighttime frontal assault on Marine positions at Alligator Creek (often called the "Ilu River" on U.S. Marine maps) on the east side of the Lunga perimeter in the early morning hours of August 21. Ichiki's assault was defeated with heavy losses for the Japanese attackers in what became known as the Battle of the Tenaru. After daybreak, the Marine units counterattacked Ichiki's surviving troops, killing many more of them, including Ichiki. In total, all but 128 of the original 917 members of the Ichiki Regiment's First Element were killed in the battle. The survivors of Ichiki's force returned to Taivu Point, notified 17th Army headquarters of their defeat in the battle, and awaited further reinforcements and orders from Rabaul.[39]

As the Tenaru battle was ending, more Japanese reinforcements were already on their way from Truk. Departing Truk on August 16 were three slow transports carrying the remaining 1,400 soldiers from Ichiki's (28th) Infantry Regiment plus 500 naval marines from the 5th Yokosuka Special Naval Landing Force.[40] Guarding the transports were 13 warships commanded by Japanese Rear Admiral Raizo Tanaka who planned to land the troops on Guadalcanal on August 24.[41] To cover the landings of these troops and provide support for the operation to retake Henderson Field from Allied forces, Yamamoto directed Chuichi Nagumo to sortie with a carrier force from Truk on August 21 and head towards the southern Solomon Islands. Nagumo's force included three carriers and 30 other warships.[42]

Simultaneously, three U.S. carrier task forces under Fletcher approached Guadalcanal to counter the Japanese offensive efforts. On August 24 and August 25, the two carrier forces fought the Battle of the Eastern Solomons, which resulted in the fleets of both adversaries retreating from the area after taking some damage, with the Japanese losing one aircraft carrier. Tanaka's convoy, after suffering heavy damage during the battle from an air attack by U.S. aircraft from Henderson Field, including the sinking of one of the transports, was forced to divert to the Shortland Islands in the northern Solomons in order for the surviving troops to be transferred to destroyers for later delivery to Guadalcanal.[43]

Throughout August, small numbers of U.S. aircraft and their crews continued to arrive at Guadalcanal. By the end of August, 64 aircraft of various types were stationed at

Henderson Field.[44] On September 3, the commander of 1st Marine Aircraft Wing, U.S. Marine Brigadier General Roy S. Geiger, arrived with his staff and took command of all air operations at Henderson Field.[45] Air battles between the Allied aircraft at Henderson and Japanese bombers and fighters from Rabaul continued almost daily. Between August 26 and September 5, the U.S. lost about 15 aircraft while the Japanese lost approximately 19 aircraft. More than half of the downed U.S. aircrews were rescued while most of the Japanese aircrews were never recovered. The eight-hour round trip flight from Rabaul to Guadalcanal, about 1,800 kilometres (1,120 miles) total, seriously hampered Japanese efforts to establish air superiority over Henderson Field. Australian coastwatchers on Bougainville and New Georgia islands were often able to provide Allied forces on Guadalcanal with advance notice of inbound Japanese air strikes, allowing the U.S. fighters time to take off and position themselves to attack the Japanese bombers and fighters as they approached Henderson Field. Thus, the Japanese air forces were slowly losing a war of attrition in the skies above Guadalcanal.[46]

During this time, Vandegrift continued to direct efforts to strengthen and improve the defenses of the Lunga perimeter. Between August 21 and September 3, he relocated three Marine battalions, including the 1st Raider Battalion, under U.S. Lieutenant Colonel Merritt A. Edson (Edson's Raiders), and the 1st Parachute Battalion from Tulagi and Gavutu to Guadalcanal. These units added about 1,500 troops to Vandegrift's original 11,000 men defending Henderson Field.[47] The 1st Parachute Battalion, which had suffered heavy casualties in the Battle of Tulagi and Gavutu-Tanambogo in August, was placed under Edson's command.[48] The other relocated battalion, the 1st Battalion, 5th Marine Regiment (1/5), was landed by boat west of the Matanikau near Kokumbuna village on August 27 with the mission of attacking Japanese units in the area, much as in the first Matanikau action of August 19. In this case, however, the U.S. Marines were impeded by difficult terrain, hot sun, and well-emplaced Japanese defenses. The next morning the Marines found that the Japanese defenders had departed during the night, so the Marines returned to the Lunga perimeter by boat.[49] Losses in this action were 20 Japanese and 3 Marines killed.[50]

Small Allied naval convoys arrived at Guadalcanal on August 23, August 29, September 1, and September 8 to provide the Marines at Lunga with more food, ammunition, aircraft fuel, and aircraft technicians. The September 1 convoy also brought 392 U.S. Navy construction engineers to maintain and improve Henderson Field.[51]

By August 23, Kawaguchi's 35th Infantry Brigade reached Truk and was loaded onto slow transport ships for the rest of the trip to Guadalcanal. The damage done to Tanaka's convoy during the Battle of the Eastern Solomons caused the Japanese to reconsider trying to deliver more troops to Guadalcanal by slow transport. Instead, the ships carrying Kawaguchi's soldiers were sent to Rabaul. From there, the Japanese planned to deliver Kawaguchi's men to Guadalcanal by destroyers staging through a Japanese naval base in the Shortland Islands. The Japanese destroyers were usually able to make round trips down "The Slot" (New Georgia Sound) to Guadalcanal and back in a single night throughout the campaign, minimizing their exposure to Allied air attack; they became known as the

"Tokyo Express" by Allied forces and "Rat Transportation" by the Japanese.[52] However, delivering the troops in this manner prevented most of the soldier's heavy equipment and supplies, such as heavy artillery, vehicles, and much food and ammunition, from being carried to Guadalcanal with them. In addition, this activity tied up destroyers the Japanese Navy desperately needed for commerce defense. Either inability or unwillingness prevented Allied naval commanders from challenging Japanese naval forces at night, so the Japanese controlled the seas around the Solomon Islands during the nighttime. However, any Japanese ship remaining within range of the aircraft at Henderson Field during the daylight hours, about 200 miles (320 km), was in great danger from damaging air attack. This "curious tactical situation" would exist for the next several months during the campaign.[53]

Between August 29 and September 4, various Japanese light cruisers, destroyers, and patrol boats were able to land almost 5,000 troops at Taivu Point, including most of the 35th Infantry Brigade, much of the Aoba (4th) Regiment, and the rest of Ichiki's regiment. General Kawaguchi, who landed at Taivu Point on the August 31 Express run, was placed in command of all the Japanese troops on Guadalcanal.[54] A barge convoy took another 1,000 soldiers of Kawaguchi's brigade, under the command of Colonel Akinosuke Oka, to Kamimbo, west of the Lunga perimeter.[55]

On September 7, Kawaguchi issued his attack plan to "rout and annihilate the enemy in the vicinity of the Guadalcanal Island airfield." Kawaguchi's attack plan called for his forces, split into three divisions, to approach the Lunga perimeter inland, culminating with a surprise night attack. Oka's forces would attack the perimeter from the west while Ichiki's Second Echelon, now renamed the Kuma Battalion, would attack from the east. The main attack would be by Kawaguchi's "Center Body," numbering 3,000 men in three battalions, from the south of the Lunga perimeter.[56] By September 7, most of Kawaguchi's troops had departed Taivu to begin marching towards Lunga Point along the coastline. About 250 Japanese troops remained behind to guard the brigade's supply base at Taivu.[57]

Meanwhile, native scouts under the direction of Martin Clemens, a coastwatcher and officer in the Solomon Islands Protectorate Defense Force, brought reports to the U.S. Marines of Japanese troops at Taivu, near the village of Tasimboko. Edson planned a raid to "wipe-out" the Japanese troop concentration at Taivu.[58] On September 8, after being dropped-off near Taivu by boat, Edson's men captured Tasimboko as the Japanese defenders retreated into the jungle.[59] In Tasimboko, Edson's troops discovered "vast stockpiles" of food, ammunition, medical supplies, and a powerful shortwave radio. After destroying everything in sight, except for some documents and equipment carried back with them, the Marines returned to the Lunga perimeter. The mounds of supplies, along with intelligence gathered from the captured documents, informed the Marines that at least 3,000 Japanese troops were on the island and apparently planning an attack on the U.S. defenses.[60]

Edson, along with Colonel Gerald Thomas, Vandegrift's operations officer, believed that the Japanese attack would come at a narrow, grassy, 1,000-yard (900 m)-long, coral ridge that paralleled the Lunga River and was located just south of Henderson Field. The ridge, called Lunga Ridge, offered a natural avenue of approach to the airfield, commanded the surrounding area and, at that time, was almost undefended. On September 11, the 840 men of Edson's battalion deployed onto and around the ridge and prepared to defend it.[61]

Oka's attacks were in the west (left), the Kuma Battalion attacked from the east (right) and the Center Body attacked "Edson's Ridge" in the lower center of the map.On the night of September 12, Kawaguchi's 1st Battalion attacked the Raiders between the Lunga River and ridge, forcing one Marine company to fall back to the ridge. The next night, Kawaguchi faced Edson's 830 Raiders with 3,000 troops of his brigade, plus an assortment of light artillery. The Japanese attack began just after nightfall, with Kawaguchi's 1st battalion assaulting Edson's right flank, just to the west of the ridge. After breaking through the Marine lines, the battalion's assault was eventually stopped by Marine units guarding the northern part of the ridge.[62]

Two companies from Kawaguchi's 2nd battalion charged up the southern edge of the ridge and pushed Edson's troops back to Hill 123 on the center part of the ridge. Throughout the night, Marines at this position, supported by artillery, defeated wave after wave of frontal Japanese attacks. Japanese units that infiltrated past the ridge to the edge of the airfield were also repulsed. Attacks by the Kuma battalion and Oka's unit at other locations on the Lunga perimeter were also defeated by the Marine defenses. On September 14, Kawaguchi led the survivors of his shattered brigade on a five day march west to the Matanikau Valley to join with Oka's unit.[63] In total, Kawaguchi's forces lost about 850 killed and the Marines 104.[64]

On September 15, General Hyakutake at Rabaul learned of Kawaguchi's defeat and forwarded the news to the Imperial General Headquarters in Japan. In an emergency session, the top Japanese army and navy command staffs concluded that, "Guadalcanal might develop into the decisive battle of the war." The results of the battle now began to have a telling strategic impact on Japanese operations in other areas of the Pacific. Hyakutake realized that in order to send sufficient troops and materiel to defeat the Allied forces on Guadalcanal, he could no longer at the same time support the major Japanese offensive currently ongoing on the Kokoda Track in New Guinea. Hyakutake, with the concurrence of the General Headquarters, ordered his troops on New Guinea, who were within 30 miles (48 km) of their objective of Port Moresby, to withdraw until the "Guadalcanal matter" was resolved. Hyakutake prepared to send more troops to Guadalcanal for another attempt to recapture Henderson Field.[65]

Reinforcements

As the Japanese regrouped west of the Matanikau, the U.S. forces concentrated on shoring up and strengthening their Lunga defenses. On September 14, Vandegrift moved another battalion, the 3rd Battalion, 2nd Marine Regiment (3/2), from Tulagi to Guadalcanal. On September 18, an Allied naval convoy delivered 4,157 men from the 3rd Provisional Marine Brigade (the U.S. 7th Marine Regiment plus a battalion from the U.S. 11th Marine Regiment and some additional support units), 137 vehicles, tents, aviation fuel, ammunition, rations, and engineering equipment to Guadalcanal. These reinforcements allowed Vandegrift, beginning on September 19, to establish an unbroken line of defense around the Lunga perimeter. While covering this convoy and herself carrying Marine replacements, the U.S. aircraft carrier Wasp was sunk by the Japanese submarine I-19 southeast of Guadalcanal, temporarily leaving only one Allied aircraft carrier (Hornet) in operation in the South Pacific area.[66] Vandegrift also made some changes in the senior leadership of his combat units, transferring off the island several officers who didn't meet his performance standards, and promoting junior officers who had "proved themselves" to take their places. One of these was the recently promoted Colonel Merritt Edson, who was placed in command of the 5th Marine Regiment.[67]

A lull occurred in the air war over Guadalcanal, with no Japanese air raids occurring between September 14 and September 27 due to bad weather, during which both sides reinforced their respective air units. The Japanese delivered 85 fighters and bombers to their air units at Rabaul while the U.S. brought 23 fighters and attack aircraft to Henderson Field. On September 20, the Japanese counted 117 total aircraft at Rabaul while the Allies tallied 71 aircraft at Henderson Field.[68] The air war resumed with a Japanese air raid on Guadalcanal on September 27, which was contested by U.S. Navy and Marine fighters from Henderson Field.[69]

The Japanese immediately began to prepare for their next attempt to recapture Henderson Field. The 3rd Battalion, 4th (Aoba) Infantry Regiment had landed at Kamimbo Bay on the western end of Guadalcanal on September 11, too late to join Kawaguchi's attack on the U.S. Marines. By now, though, the battalion had joined Oka's forces near the Matanikau. Tokyo Express runs by destroyers on September 14, 20, 21, and 24 brought food and ammunition, as well as 280 men from the 1st Battalion, Aoba Regiment, to Kamimbo on Guadalcanal. The Japanese 2nd Infantry Division was transported from the Dutch East Indies to Rabaul beginning on September 13 and prepared for transport by Tokyo Express to Guadalcanal. Much of the Japanese 38th Division, also in the Dutch East Indies, followed the 2nd to Rabaul in preparation for deployment to Guadalcanal. The Japanese planned to transport a total of 17,500 troops from the 2nd and 38th Divisions to the island to take part in the next major attack on the Lunga Perimeter, set for October 20, 1942.[70]

General Vandegrift and his staff were aware that Kawaguchi's troops had retreated to the area west of the Matanikau and that numerous groups of Japanese stragglers were scattered throughout the area between the Lunga Perimeter and the Matanikau River. Vandegrift, therefore, decided to conduct another series of small unit operations around the Matanikau Valley. The purpose of these operations was to "mop-up" the scattered groups of Japanese troops east of the Matanikau and to keep the main body of Japanese soldiers off-balance to prevent them from consolidating their positions so close to the main Marine defenses at Lunga Point.[71]

The first U.S. Marine operation and attempt to attack Japanese forces west of the Matanikau, conducted between September 23 and September 27, 1942 by elements of three U.S. Marine battalions, was repulsed by Kawaguchi's troops under Akinosuke Oka's local command. During the action, three U.S. Marine companies were surrounded by Japanese forces near Point Cruz west of the Matanikau, took heavy losses, and barely escaped with assistance from a U.S. Navy destroyer and landing craft manned by U.S. Coast Guard personnel.[72]

In the second action between October 6 and 9, a larger force of U.S. Marines successfully crossed the Matanikau River, attacked newly landed Japanese forces from the 2nd Infantry Division under the command of generals Masao Maruyama and Yumio Nasu, and inflicted heavy losses on the Japanese 4th Infantry Regiment. The second action forced the Japanese to retreat from their positions east of the Matanikau and hindered Japanese preparations for their planned major offensive on the U.S. Lunga defenses set for later in October, 1942.[73]

Between October 9 and October 11 the U.S. 1st Battalion 2nd Marines raided two small Japanese outposts about 30 miles (48 km) east of the Lunga perimeter at Gurabusu and Koilotumaria near Aola Bay. The raids killed 35 Japanese at a cost of 17 Marines and three U.S. Navy personnel killed. [74]

Battle of Cape Esperance

Throughout the last week of September and the first week of October, Tokyo Express runs delivered troops from the Japanese 2nd Infantry Division to Guadalcanal. The Japanese Navy promised to support the Army's planned offensive by not only delivering the necessary troops, equipment, and supplies to the island, but by stepping-up air attacks on Henderson Field and sending warships to bombard the airfield.[75]

In the meantime, Major General Millard F. Harmon, commander of United States Army forces in the South Pacific, convinced Ghormley that U.S. Marine forces on Guadalcanal needed to be reinforced immediately if the Allies were to successfully defend the island from the next, expected Japanese offensive. Thus, on October 8, the 2,837 men of the 164th Infantry Regiment from the U.S. Army's American Division boarded ships at New Caledonia for the trip to Guadalcanal with a projected arrival date of October 13. To protect the transports carrying the 164th to Guadalcanal, Ghormley ordered Task Force 64, consisting of four cruisers and five destroyers under U.S. Rear Admiral Norman Scott, to intercept and combat any Japanese ships that approached Guadalcanal and threatened the arrival of the transport convoy.[76]

Mikawa's Eighth Fleet staff scheduled a large and "singularly important" Tokyo Express supply run for the night of October 11. Two seaplane tenders and six destroyers were to deliver 728 soldiers plus artillery and ammunition to Guadalcanal. At the same time but in a separate operation three heavy cruisers and two destroyers under the command of Rear Admiral Aritomo Gotō were to bombard Henderson Field with special explosive shells with the object of destroying the CAF and the airfield's facilities. Due to the fact that U.S. Navy warships had yet to attempt to interdict any Tokyo Express missions to Guadalcanal, the Japanese weren't expecting any opposition from naval surface forces that night.[77]

Just before midnight, Scott's warships detected Gotō's force on radar near the entrance to the strait between Savo Island and Guadalcanal. By happenstance, Scott's force was in a position to cross the T of Gotō's unsuspecting formation. Opening fire, Scott's warships sank one of Gotō's cruisers and one of his destroyers, heavily damaged another cruiser, mortally wounded Gotō, and forced the rest of Gotō's warships to abandon the bombardment mission and retreat. During the exchange of gunfire, one of Scott's destroyers was sunk and one cruiser and another destroyer were heavily damaged. In the meantime, the Japanese supply convoy successfully completed unloading at Guadalcanal and began its return journey without being discovered by Scott's force. Later on the morning of October 12, four Japanese destroyers from the supply convoy turned back to assist Gotō's retreating, damaged warships. Air attacks by CAF aircraft from Henderson Field sank two of these destroyers later that day. The convoy of U.S. Army troops reached Guadalcanal as scheduled the next day.[78]

Battleship bombardment of Henderson Field

In spite of the U.S. victory off Cape Esperance, the Japanese continued with plans and preparations for their large offensive scheduled for later in October. The Japanese decided to risk a one-time departure from their usual practice of only using fast warships to deliver their men and materiel to the island. On October 13 a convoy comprising six cargo ships with eight screening destroyers departed the Shortland Islands for Guadalcanal. The convoy carried 4,500 troops from the 16th and 230th Infantry Regiments, some naval marines, two batteries of heavy artillery and one company of tanks.[79]

To protect the approaching convoy from attack by CAF aircraft, Yamamoto sent two battleships from Truk to bombard Henderson Field. At 01:33 on October 14 the Japanese battleships Kongō and Haruna, escorted by one light cruiser and nine destroyers, approached Guadalcanal and opened fire on Henderson Field from a distance of 16,000 metres (17,000 yd). Over the next one hour and 23 minutes, the two battleships fired 973 14-inch (360 mm) shells into the Lunga perimeter, most of them falling in and around the 2,200-meter-square area of the airfield. The bombardment heavily damaged both runways, burned almost all of the available aviation fuel, destroyed 48 of the CAF's 90 aircraft, and killed 41 men, including six CAF pilots.[80]

In spite of the heavy damage, Henderson personnel were able to restore one of the runways to operational condition within a few hours. Seventeen SBDs and 20 Wildcats at Espiritu Santo were immediately flown to Henderson and U.S. Army and Marine transport aircraft began to shuttle aviation gasoline from Espiritu Santo to Guadalcanal. Now aware of the approach of the large Japanese reinforcement convoy, the U.S. desperately sought some way to interdict the convoy before it could reach Guadalcanal. Using fuel drained from destroyed aircraft and fuel from a safe cache in the nearby jungle, the CAF attacked the convoy twice on the 14th, but caused no damage.[81]

Since arriving on Guadalcanal, Colonel Woods, Chief of Staff, 1st Marine Aircraft Wing, had padded expenditures in order to accelerate the forwarding of more fuel supplies. Due to Colonel Woods' proactive measure, Henderson Field enjoyed a sizable emergency reserve of fuel. The reserve fuel arriving on the 'canal was not being located in "safe caches" but was being stockpiled alongside the airstrip in order to refuel the aircraft faster. Just days before the October 14 naval bombardment, Navy sailor August Martello, acting on a hunch, led a working party in the movement of 488 fifty-five gallon drums of aviation gas to the relative security of the jungle canopy safely away from Henderson Field as a precautionary measure. That surviving cache of fuel enabled the CAF aircrews on Guadalcanal to continue flying vital missions against the enemy until desperately needed supplies began to arrive. [82]

The Japanese convoy reached Tassafaronga on Guadalcanal at midnight on October 14 and began unloading. Throughout the day of October 15, a string of CAF aircraft from Henderson bombed and strafed the unloading convoy, destroying three of the cargo ships. The remainder of the convoy departed that night, having unloaded all of the troops and about two-thirds of the supplies and equipment. Several Japanese heavy cruisers also bombarded Henderson on the nights of October 14 and 15, destroying additional CAF aircraft, but failing to cause significant further damage to the airfield.[83]

Battle for Henderson Field

Between October 1 and October 17, the Japanese had delivered 15,000 troops to Guadalcanal, giving Hyakutake 20,000 total troops to employ for his planned offensive. Because of the loss of their positions on the east side of the Matanikau, the Japanese decided that an attack on the U.S. defenses along the coast would be prohibitively difficult.

Therefore, Hyakutake decided that the main thrust of his planned attack would be from south of Henderson Field. His 2nd Division (augmented by troops from the 38th Division), under Lieutenant General Masao Maruyama and comprising 7,000 soldiers in three infantry regiments of three battalions each was ordered to march through the jungle and attack the American defences from the south near the east bank of the Lunga River.[84] The date of the attack was set for October 22. To distract the Americans from the planned attack from the south, Hyakutake's heavy artillery plus five battalions of infantry (about 2,900 men) under Major General Tadashi Sumiyoshi were to attack the American defenses from the west along the coastal corridor. The Japanese estimated that there were 10,000 American troops on the island, when in fact there were about 23,000.[85]

On October 12, a company of Japanese engineers began to break a trail, called the "Maruyama Road", from the Matanikau towards the southern portion of the U.S. Lunga perimeter. The 15 miles (24 km) long trail traversed some of the most difficult terrain on Guadalcanal, including numerous rivers and streams, deep, muddy ravines, steep ridges, and dense jungle. Between October 16 and October 18, the 2nd Division began their march along the Maruyama Road.[86]

By October 23, Maruyama's forces still struggled through the jungle to reach the American lines. That evening, after learning that his forces had yet to reach the American lines, Hyakutake postponed the attack to 19:00 on October 24. The Americans remained completely unaware of the approach of Maruyama's forces.[87]

Sumiyoshi was informed by Hyakutake's staff of the postponement of the offensive to October 24, but was unable to contact his troops to inform them of the delay. Thus, at dusk on October 23, two battalions of the 4th Infantry Regiment and the nine tanks of the 1st Independent Tank Company launched attacks on the U.S. Marine defenses at the mouth of the Matanikau. U.S. Marine artillery, cannon, and small arms fire repulsed the attacks, destroying all the tanks and killing many of the Japanese soldiers while suffering only light casualties to themselves.[88]

Finally, late on October 24 Maruyama's forces reached the U.S. Lunga perimeter. Over two consecutive nights Maruyama's forces conducted numerous, unsuccessful frontal assaults on positions defended by troops of the 1st Battalion, 7th Marines under Lieutenant Colonel Chesty Puller and the 3rd Battalion, 164th Infantry Regiment, commanded by Lieutenant Colonel Robert Hall. U.S. Marine and Army rifle, machine gun, mortar, artillery and direct canister fire from 37 mm anti-tank guns "wrought terrible carnage" on the Japanese.[89] A few small groups of Japanese broke through the American defenses, but were all hunted down and killed over the next several days. More than 1,500 of Maruyama's troops were killed in the attacks while the Americans lost about 60 killed. Over the same two days American aircraft from Henderson Field defended against attacks by Japanese aircraft and ships, destroying 14 aircraft and sinking a light cruiser.[90]

Further Japanese attacks near the Matanikau on October 26 were also repulsed with heavy losses for the Japanese. Thus, at 08:00 on October 26, Hyakutake called off any further attacks and ordered his forces to retreat. About half of Maruyama's survivors were ordered to retreat back to the upper Matanikau Valley while the 230th Infantry Regiment under Colonel Toshinari Shoji was told to head for Koli Point, east of the Lunga perimeter. Leading elements of the 2nd Division reached the 17th Army headquarters area at Kokumbona, west of the Matanikau on November 4. The same day, Shoji's unit reached Koli Point and made camp. Decimated by battle deaths, combat injuries, malnutrition, and tropical diseases, the 2nd Division was incapable of further offensive action and would fight as a defensive force along the coast for the rest of the campaign. In total the Japanese lost 2,200 – 3,000 troops in the battle while the Americans lost around 80 killed.[91]

Battle of the Santa Cruz Islands

At the same time that Hyakutake's troops were attacking the Lunga perimeter, Japanese aircraft carriers and other large warships under the overall direction of Isoroku Yamamoto moved into a position near the southern Solomon Islands. From this location, the Japanese naval forces hoped to engage and decisively defeat any Allied (primarily U.S.) naval forces, especially carrier forces, that responded to Hyakutake's ground offensive. Allied naval carrier forces in the area, now under the overall command of William Halsey, Jr. who had replaced Ghormley on October 18, also hoped to meet the Japanese naval forces in battle. Nimitz had replaced Ghormley with Halsey after concluding that Ghormley had become too pessimistic and myopic to effectively continue leading Allied forces in the South Pacific area.[92]

The two opposing carrier forces confronted each other on the morning of October 26, in what became known as the Battle of the Santa Cruz Islands. After an exchange of carrier air attacks, Allied surface ships were forced to retreat from the battle area with the loss of one carrier sunk (Hornet) and another (Enterprise) heavily damaged. The participating Japanese carrier forces, however, also retreated because of high aircraft and aircrew losses and significant damage to two carriers. Although an apparent tactical victory for the Japanese in terms of ships sunk and damaged, the loss by the Japanese of many irreplaceable, veteran aircrews provided a long-term strategic advantage for the Allies, whose aircrew losses in the battle were relatively low.[93]

November land actions

In order to exploit the victory in the Battle for Henderson Field, Vandegrift sent six Marine battalions, later joined by one US Army battalion, on an offensive west of the Matanikau. The operation was commanded by Merritt Edson and its goal was to capture Kokumbona, headquarters of the 17th Army, west of Point Cruz. Defending the Point Cruz area were Japanese army troops from the 4th Infantry Regiment commanded by Nomasu Nakaguma. The 4th Infantry was severely understrength because of battle damage, tropical disease, and malnutrition.[94]

The American offensive began on November 1 and, after some difficulty, succeeded in destroying Japanese forces defending the Point Cruz area by November 3, including rear echelon troops sent to reinforce Nakaguma's battered regiment. The Americans appeared to be on the verge of breaking through the Japanese defenses and capturing Kokumbona. At this time, however, other American forces discovered and engaged newly landed Japanese troops near Koli Point on the eastern side of the Lunga perimeter. To counter this new threat, Vandegrift temporarily halted the Matanikau offensive on November 4. The Americans suffered 71 and the Japanese around 400 killed in the offensive.[95]

At Koli Point early in the morning November 3, five Japanese destroyers delivered 300 army troops to support Shōji and his troops who were enroute to Koli Point after the Battle for Henderson Field. Having learned of the planned landing, Vandegrift sent a battalion of Marines under Herman H. Hanneken to intercept the Japanese at Koli. Soon after landing, the Japanese soldiers encountered and drove Hanneken's battalion back towards the Lunga perimeter. In response, Vandegrift ordered Puller's Marine battalion plus two of the 164th infantry battalions, along with Hanneken's battalion, to move towards Koli Point to attack the Japanese forces there.[96]

As the American troops began to move, Shōji and his soldiers began to arrive at Koli Point. Beginning on November 8, the American troops attempted to encircle Shōji's forces at Gavaga Creek near Koli Point. Meanwhile, Hyakutake ordered Shōji to abandon his positions at Koli and rejoin Japanese forces at Kokumbona in the Matanikau area. A gap existed by way of a swampy creek in the southern side of the American lines. Between November 9 and 11, Shōji and between 2,000 and 3,000 of his men escaped into the jungle to the south. On November 12, the Americans completely overran and killed all the remaining Japanese soldiers left in the pocket. The Americans counted the bodies of 450–475 Japanese dead in the Koli Point area and captured most of Shōji's heavy weapons and provisions. The American forces suffered 40 killed and 120 wounded in the operation.[97]

Meanwhile, on November 4, two companies from the 2nd Marine Raider Battalion, commanded by Lieutenant Colonel Evans Carlson landed by boat at Aola Bay, 40 miles (64 km) east of Lunga Point. Carlson's raiders, along with troops from the US Army's 147th Infantry Regiment, were to provide security for 500 Seabees as they attempted to construct an airfield at that location. Halsey, acting on a recommendation by Rear Admiral Richmond K. Turner, US naval commander of amphibious forces for the south Pacific, had approved the Aola Bay airfield construction effort.[98]

On November 5, Vandegrift ordered Carlson to take his raiders, march overland from Aola, and attack any of Shōji's forces that escaped from Koli Point. With the rest of the companies from his battalion, which arrived a few days later, Carlson and his troops set off on a 29-day patrol from Aola to the Lunga perimeter. During the patrol, the raiders fought several battles with Shōji's retreating forces, killing almost 500 of them, while suffering 16 killed themselves. In addition to the losses sustained from attacks by Carlson's raiders, tropical diseases and a lack of food felled many more of Shōji's men. By the time Shōji's forces reached the Lunga River in mid-November, about halfway to the Matanikau, only 1,300 men remained with the main body. When Shōji reached the 17th Army positions west of the Matanikau, only 700 to 800 survivors were still with him.

Seriously weakened by their ordeal, Shōji's men played little part in the remainder of the campaign.[99]

Tokyo Express runs on November 5, 7, and 9 delivered additional troops from the Japanese 38th Infantry Division, including most of the 228th Infantry Regiment to Guadalcanal. These fresh troops were quickly emplaced in the Point Cruz and Matanikau area and helped successfully resist further attacks by American forces on November 10 and 18. The Americans and Japanese would remain facing each other along a line just west of Point Cruz for the next six weeks.[100]

Naval Battle of Guadalcanal

After the defeat in the Battle for Henderson Field, the Japanese army planned to try again to retake the airfield in November 1942, but further reinforcements were needed before the operation could proceed. The army requested assistance from Yamamoto to deliver the needed reinforcements to the island and to support the next offensive. Yamamoto provided 11 large transport ships to carry 7,000 army troops from the 38th Infantry Division, their ammunition, food, and heavy equipment from Rabaul to Guadalcanal. He also provided a warship support force that included two battleships. The two battleships, Hiei and Kirishima, equipped with special fragmentation shells, were to bombard Henderson Field on the night of November 12 — 13 and destroy it and the aircraft stationed there in order to allow the slow, heavy transports to reach Guadalcanal and unload safely the next day.[101] The warship force was commanded from Hiei by recently-promoted Vice Admiral Hiroaki Abe.[102]

In early November, Allied intelligence learned that the Japanese were preparing again to try to retake Henderson Field.[103] Therefore, the U.S. sent Task Force 67, a large reinforcement and resupply convoy carrying Marine replacements, two US Army infantry battalions, and ammunition and food, commanded by Rear Admiral Richmond K. Turner, to Guadalcanal on November 11. The supply ships were protected by two task groups, commanded by Rear Admirals Daniel J. Callaghan and Norman Scott, and aircraft from Henderson Field.[104] The ships were attacked several times on November 11 and November 12 by Japanese aircraft based at Buin, Bougainville, in the Solomons, but most were unloaded without serious damage.[105]

U.S. reconnaissance aircraft spotted the approach of Abe's bombardment force and passed a warning to the Allied command.[106] Thus warned, Turner detached all usable combat ships under Callaghan to protect the troops ashore from the expected Japanese naval attack and troop landing and ordered the supply ships at Guadalcanal to depart by early evening November 12.[107] Callaghan's force comprised two heavy cruisers, three light cruisers, and eight destroyers.[108]

Around 01:30 on November 13, Callaghan's force intercepted Abe's bombardment group between Guadalcanal and Savo Island. In addition to the two battleships, Abe's force included one light cruiser and 11 destroyers. In the pitch darkness,[109] the two warship forces intermingled before opening fire at unusually close distances. In the resulting melée, Abe's warships sunk or severely damaged all but one cruiser and one destroyer in Callaghan's force and killed

Callaghan. Two Japanese destroyers were sunk and another destroyer and Hiei were heavily damaged. In spite of his overwhelming defeat of Callaghan's force, Abe ordered his warships to retire without bombarding Henderson Field. Hiei sank later that day after repeated air attacks by CAF aircraft and aircraft from the US carrier Enterprise. Because of Abe's failure to neutralize Henderson Field, Yamamoto ordered the troop transport convoy, under the command of Raizo Tanaka and located near the Shortland Islands, to wait an additional day before heading towards Guadalcanal. Yamamoto ordered Nobutake Kondo to assemble another bombardment force to attack Henderson Field and to protect the expected arrival and offloading of the transport ships at Guadalcanal on November 15.[110]

In the meantime, around 02:00 on November 14, a cruiser and destroyer force under Gunichi Mikawa from Rabaul conducted an unopposed bombardment of Henderson Field. The bombardment caused some damage but failed to put the airfield or most of its aircraft out of operation. As Mikawa's force retired towards Rabaul, Tanaka's transport convoy, trusting that Henderson Field was now destroyed or heavily damaged, began its run down the slot towards Guadalcanal. Throughout the day of November 14, aircraft from Henderson Field and Enterprise attacked Mikawa's and Tanaka's ships, sinking one heavy cruiser and seven of the transports. Most of the troops were rescued from the transports by Tanaka's escorting destroyers and returned to the Shortlands. After dark, the remaining four transports continued towards Guadalcanal as Kondo's force approached to bombard Henderson Field.[111]

In order to intercept Kondo's force, Halsey, who was low on undamaged ships, detached two battleships, Washington and South Dakota, and four destroyers from the Enterprise task force. The U.S. force, under the command of Willis A. Lee on Washington, reached Guadalcanal and Savo Island just before midnight on November 14, shortly before Kondo's bombardment force arrived. Kondo's force consisted of Kirishima plus two heavy cruisers, two light cruisers, and nine destroyers. After the two forces made contact, Kondo's force quickly sank three of the four US destroyers and heavily damaged the fourth. The Japanese warships then sighted, opened fire, and damaged South Dakota. As Kondo's warships concentrated on South Dakota, Washington approached the Japanese ships unobserved and opened fire on Kirishima, hitting the Japanese battleship repeatedly and causing fatal damage. After fruitlessly chasing Washington towards the Russell Islands, Kondo ordered his warships to retire without bombarding Henderson Field. One of Kondo's destroyers was also sunk during the engagement.[112]

As Kondo's ships retired, the four Japanese transports beached themselves near Tassafaronga on Guadalcanal at 04:00 and quickly began unloading. At 05:55 U.S. aircraft and artillery began attacking the beached transports, destroying all four transports along with most of the supplies that they carried. Only 2,000–3,000 of the army troops made it ashore. Because of the failure to deliver most of the troops and supplies, the Japanese were forced to cancel their planned November offensive on Henderson Field.[113]

On November 26, Japanese Lieutenant General Hitoshi Imamura took command of the newly formed Eighth Area Army at Rabaul. The new command encompassed both Hyakutake's 17th Army and the 18th Army in New Guinea. One of Imamura's first priorities upon assuming command was the continuation of the attempts to retake Henderson Field and Guadalcanal. The Allied offensive at Buna in New Guinea, however, changed Imamura's priorities. Because the Allied attempt to take Buna was considered a more severe threat to Rabaul, Imamura postponed further major reinforcement efforts to Guadalcanal to concentrate on the situation in New Guinea.[114]

Battle of Tassafaronga

The Japanese continued to experience problems in delivering sufficient supplies to sustain their troops on Guadalcanal. Attempts to use only submarines the last two weeks in November failed to provide sufficient food for Hyakutake's forces. A separate attempt to establish bases in the central Solomons to facilitate barge convoys to Guadalcanal also failed because of destructive Allied air attacks. On November 26, the 17th Army notified Imamura that it faced a critical food crisis. Some front-line units had not been resupplied for six days and even the rear-area troops were on one-third rations. The situation forced the Japanese to return to using destroyers to deliver the necessary supplies.[115]

Eighth Fleet personnel devised a plan to help reduce the exposure of destroyers delivering supplies to Guadalcanal. Large oil or gas drums were cleaned and filled with medical supplies and food, with enough air space to provide buoyancy, and strung together with rope. When the destroyers arrived at Guadalcanal they would make a sharp turn and the drums would be cut loose and a swimmer or boat from shore could pick up the buoyed end of a rope and return it to the beach, where the soldiers could haul in the supplies.[116]

The Eighth Fleet's Guadalcanal Reinforcement Unit (the Tokyo Express), currently commanded by Rear Admiral Raizo Tanaka, was tasked by Mikawa with making the first of five scheduled runs to Tassafaronga on Guadalcanal using the drum method on the night of November 30. Tanaka's unit was centered around eight destroyers, with six destroyers assigned to carry between 200 to 240 drums of supplies apiece.[117] Notified by intelligence sources of the Japanese supply attempt, Halsey ordered the newly formed Task Force 67, comprising four cruisers and four destroyers under the command of US Rear Admiral Carleton H. Wright, to intercept Tanaka's force off Guadalcanal. Two additional destroyers joined Wright's force enroute to Guadalcanal from Espiritu Santo during the day of November 30.[118]

At 22:40 on November 30, Tanaka's force arrived off Guadalcanal and prepared to unload the supply barrels. Meanwhile, Wright's warships were approaching through Ironbottom Sound from the opposite direction. Wright's van destroyers detected Tanaka's force on radar and the destroyer commander requested permission to attack with torpedoes. Wright waited four minutes before giving permission, allowing Tanaka's force to escape from an optimum firing setup. All of the American torpedoes missed their targets. At the same time, Wright's cruisers opened fire, quickly hitting and destroying one of the Japanese guard destroyers. The rest of Tanaka's warships abandoned the supply mission, increased speed, turned, and launched a total of 44 torpedoes in the direction of Wright's cruisers.[119]

The Japanese torpedoes hit and sank the US cruiser Northampton and heavily damaged the cruisers Minneapolis, New Orleans, and Pensacola. The rest of Tanaka's destroyers escaped without damage, but failed to deliver any of the provisions to Guadalcanal.[120]

By December 7, 1942, Hyakutake's forces were losing about 50 men each day from malnutrition, disease, and Allied ground or air attacks.[121] Further attempts by Tanaka's force to deliver provisions on December 3, 7, and 11 failed to alleviate the crisis, and one of Tanaka's destroyers was sunk by a US PT boat torpedo.[122]

On December 12, the Japanese Navy proposed that Guadalcanal be abandoned. Despite opposition from Japanese Army leaders, who still hoped that Guadalcanal could eventually be retaken from the Allies, Japan's Imperial General Headquarters, with approval from the Emperor, on December 31, 1942, agreed to the evacuation of all Japanese forces from the island and establishment of a new line of defense for the Solomons on New Georgia. The Japanese secretly began to prepare for the evacuation, called Operation Ke, scheduled to begin during the latter part of January 1943.[123]

Final Allied offensives and Operation Ke

By December the weary 1st Marine Division was withdrawn for recuperation, and over the course of the next month the U.S. XIV Corps took over operations on the island. This corps consisted of the 2nd Marine Division and the U.S. Army's 25th Infantry and Americal Divisions. A division-sized task force of Army and Marine Corps units combined to form the unofficial "Composite Army-Marine Division" ("CAM Division"), consisting of the 6th Marines, 147th and 182nd Infantry, and the division staff of the 2nd Marine Division.

The U.S. XIV Corps began final offensive operations on 10 January 1943, and pushed the remaining Japanese forces westward towards Cape Esperance. The last Japanese resistance in the Guadalcanal campaign ended on February 9, 1943, with the successful evacuation of most of the surviving Japanese troops from the island by the Japanese navy in Operation Ke.[124]

Aftermath and historical significance

The Battle of Midway is widely considered to be the turning point in the Pacific theater, as it was a strategic naval victory which stopped Japan's eastern expansion toward Hawaii and the U.S. west coast. However, the Empire of Japan continued to expand in the southern Pacific, until receiving two decisive defeats at the hands of the Allies. Australian land forces had defeated Japanese Marines in New Guinea at the Battle of Milne Bay in September 1942, which was the first land defeat suffered by the Japanese in the Pacific. And, by the end of 1942, it was clear that Japan also had lost the Guadalcanal campaign, a more serious blow to Japan's strategic plans and an unanticipated defeat at the hands of the Americans.

The Guadalcanal campaign was costly to Japan strategically and in material losses and manpower. Roughly 30,000 Japanese troops were killed during the campaign. Japan lost control of the Solomons Islands and the ability to interdict Allied shipping to Australia. Japan's major base at Rabaul was now directly threatened by Allied air power. Most importantly, scarce Japanese land, air, and naval forces had disappeared forever into the Guadalcanal jungle and surrounding sea. The Japanese aircraft and ships destroyed and sunk in this campaign were irreplaceable, as were their highly-trained and veteran crews. It thus can be argued that this Allied victory was the first step in a long string of successes that eventually led to the surrender of Japan and the occupation of the Japanese home islands.

The Battle of Guadalcanal was one of the first prolonged campaigns in the Pacific. The campaign was a battle of attrition that strained the logistical capabilities of both sides. For the U.S. this need prompted the development of effective combat air transport for the first time. Japan was forced to rely on reinforcement by barges, destroyers, and submarines, with very uneven results. Early in the campaign, the Americans were hindered by a lack of resources due to the "Germany First" policy of the United States. However, as the campaign continued, and the American public became more and more aware of the plight and perceived heroism of the American forces on Guadalcanal, more forces were dispatched to the area. This spelled trouble for Japan as its military-industrial complex was unable to match the output of American industry and manpower. Thus, as the campaign wore on the Japanese were losing irreplaceable units while the Americans were rapidly replacing and even augmenting their forces.

After Guadalcanal the Japanese were clearly on the defensive in the Pacific. The constant pressure to reinforce Guadalcanal had weakened Japanese efforts in other theatres, contributing to a successful Australian counteroffensive in New Guinea which culminated in the capture of the key bases of Buna and Gona in early 1943. In June, the Allies launched Operation Cartwheel, which initiated a strategy of isolating the major Japanese forward base, at Rabaul, and concentrated on cutting its sea lines of communication. This prepared the way for the island hopping campaigns of General Douglas MacArthur in the South West Pacific and Admiral Chester Nimitz in the Central Pacific; both efforts advancing toward Japan.

According to U.S. historian Gerhard L. Weinberg, Guadalcanal's broader effect on the war has often been overlooked. Japan's leaders planned a major offensive in the Indian Ocean and so notified their German ally, but the ships and planes required for the undertaking were instead drained into the Guadalcanal quagmire. Indeed, losses there undermined Japan's "barrier" defense.[125] At the time Guadalcanal began, British Commonwealth forces were struggling to hold the German Afrika Korps away from the Suez Canal. Resupply and reinforcements which contributed to the victory at El Alamein were sent because the Indian Ocean was open to Allied shipping. [126] In addition, vital Lend-Lease supplies from the U.S. were able to travel through the Indian Ocean and across Iran just as the Soviet Union was struggling to defeat

Germany's Fall Blau. British power in India itself was at its weakest in 1942; Japan's one and only chance of toppling the Raj, and severing the last supply routes to Nationalist China, slipped away in the Southwest Pacific.[127]

Notes

1. Zimmerman, *The Guadalcanal Campaign*, p. 173–175 documents the participation by native Solomon Islanders in the campaign [1]. Guadalcanal and the rest of the Solomon Islands were technically under UK/Australian political control during World War II.

2. Vava'u Press Ltd, *Matangi Tonga Online*, 2006 [2] states that 28 Tongan soldiers fought on Guadalcanal, with two of them killed in action.

3. Frank, *Guadalcanal*, p. 57, 619–621; and Rottman, *Japanese Army*, p. 64. Approximately 20,000 U.S. Marines and 40,000 U.S. Army troops were deployed on Guadalcanal at different times during the campaign.

4. Rottman, *Japanese Army*, p. 65. 31,400 Imperial Japanese Army and 4,800 Imperial Japanese Navy troops were deployed to Guadalcanal during the campaign.

5. Frank, *Guadalcanal*, p. 598–618; and Lundstrom, *Guadalcanal campaign*, p. 456. Numbers include

personnel killed by all causes including combat, disease, and accidents. Four U.S. aircrew were captured by the Japanese during the Battle of the Santa Cruz Islands and survived their captivity. An unknown number of other U.S. ground and aircrew personnel were, according to Japanese records, captured by Japanese forces during the campaign but did not survive their captivity. Ships sunk includes both warships and "large" auxiliaries. Aircraft destroyed includes both combat and operational losses.

6. Frank, *Guadalcanal*, p. 598–618; and Rottman, *Japanese Army*, p. 65. Numbers include personnel killed by all causes including combat, disease, and accidents. Approximately 9,000 died from disease. Most of the captured personnel were Korean laborers assigned to Japanese naval construction units. Ships sunk includes warships and "large" auxiliaries. Aircraft destroyed includes both combat and operational losses.

7. Murray, *War to be Won*, p. 169–195.

8. Murray, *War to be Won*, p. 196.

9. Loxton, *Shame of Savo*, p. 3.

10. Frank, *Guadalcanal*, p. 23–31, 129, 628; Smith, *Bloody Ridge*, p. 5; and Lundstrom, *Guadalcanal Campaign*, p. 39.

11. Morison, *Struggle for Guadalcanal*, p. 12.

12. Murray, *War to be Won*, p. 199–200; Jersey, *Hell's Islands*, p. 85; and Lundstrom, *Guadalcanal Campaign*, p. 5.

13. Loxton, *Shame of Savo*, p. 5; and Miller, *Cactus Air Force*, p. 11.

14. Frank, *Guadalcanal*, p. 35–37, 53.

15. Morison, *Struggle for Guadalcanal*, p. 15; and McGee, *The Solomons Campaigns*, p. 20–21.

16. Frank, *Guadalcanal*, p. 57, 619–621.

17. McGee, *The Solomons Campaigns*, p. 21.

18. Frank, *Guadalcanal*, p. 60; Jersey, *Hell's Islands*, p. 95. The landing force, designated Task Force 62, included six heavy cruisers, two light cruisers, 15 destroyers, 13 transports, six cargo ships, four destroyer transports, and five minesweepers.

19. Hammel, *Carrier Clash*, p. 46–47; and Lundstrom, *Guadalcanal Campaign*, p. 38.

20. Frank, *Guadalcanal*, p. 51.

21. Frank, *Guadalcanal*, p. 50.

22. Shaw, *First Offensive*, p. 8–9; and McGee, *The Solomons Campaigns*, p. 32–34.

23. Frank, *Guadalcanal*, p. 79. Approximately 80 Japanese personnel escaped from the islands to Florida Island, where they were found and killed by Marine patrols over the next two months.

24. Jersey, *Hell's Islands*, p. 113–115, 190; Morison, *Struggle for Guadalcanal*, p. 15; and Frank, *Guadalcanal*, p. 61–62 & 81.

25. Loxton, *Shame of Savo*, pp. 90–103.

26. Frank, *Guadalcanal*, p. 80.

27. Hammel, *Carrier Clash*, p. 99; and Loxton, *Shame of Savo*, pp. 104–5. Loxton, Frank (*Guadalcanal* p. 94), and Morison (*Struggle for Guadalcanal*, p. 28) contend Fletcher's fuel situation was not at all critical, but Fletcher implied it was in order to provide further justification for his withdrawal from the battle area.

28. Hammel, *Carrier Clash*, p. 100.

29. Morison, *Struggle for Guadalcanal* p. 31.

30. Morison, *Struggle for Guadalcanal*, p. 19–59.

31. Smith, *Bloody Ridge*, p. 14–15. At this time there were exactly 10,819 Marines on Guadalcanal, *Guadalcanal*, p. 125–127.

32. Smith, *Bloody Ridge*, p. 16–17.

33. Shaw, *First Offensive*, p. 13.

34. Smith, *Bloody Ridge*, p. 20, 35–36.

35. Zimmerman, *The Guadalcanal Campaign*, p. 58–60; Smith, *Bloody Ridge*, p. 35; and Jersey, *Hell's Islands*, p. 196–199. Only three made it back to the Lunga Point perimeter. Goettge was one of the first killed. Seven Japanese were killed in the skirmish. More details of the event are at: [3], [4], [5], [6], [7], and [8].

36. Frank, *Guadalcanal*, p. 132–133; Jersey, *Hell's Islands*, p. 203; and Smith, *Bloody Ridge*, p. 36–42. The 500 Japanese personnel involved in this engagement were from the 84th Guard Unit, 11th and 13th Construction Unit, and the recently arrived 1st Camp Relief Unit. After this

engagement, the Japanese naval personnel relocated deeper into the hills in the interior of the island.

37. Shaw, *First Offensive*, p. 18.

38. Smith, *Bloody Ridge*, p. 88; Evans, *Japanese Navy*, p. 158; and Frank, *Guadalcanal*, p. 141–143. The Ichiki regiment was named after its commanding officer. The Aoba regiment took its name from Aoba Castle in Sendai, because most of the soldiers in the regiment were from Miyagi prefecture (Rottman, *Japanese Army*, p. 52). Although some histories state that Ichiki's regiment was at Truk, Raizo Tanaka, in Evans' book, states that he dropped off Ichiki's regiment at Guam after the Battle of Midway. Ichiki's regiment was subsequently loaded on ships for transport elsewhere but were rerouted to Truk after the Allied landings.

39. Frank, *Guadalcanal*, p. 156–158 & 681; and Smith, *Bloody Ridge*, p. 43.

40. Smith, *Bloody Ridge*, p. 33–34.

41. Zimmerman, *The Guadalcanal Campaign*, p. 70; and Frank, *Guadalcanal*, p. 159.

42. Hammel, *Carrier Clash*, 124–125, 157.

43. Hara, *Japanese Destroyer Captain*, 118–119; and Hough, *Pearl Harbor to Guadalcanal*, p. 293. An unknown, but "large" number of the 5th Yokosuka troops were killed in the sinking of their transport ship.

44. Zimmerman, *The Guadalcanal Campaign*, p. 74.

45. Hough, *Pearl Harbor to Guadalcanal*, p. 297.

46. Frank, *Guadalcanal*, p. 194–213; and Lundstrom, *Guadalcanal Campaign*, p. 45. In comparison to the 560 miles (900 km) separating Lunga Point from Rabaul, Berlin was about 460 miles (740 km) from Allied air bases in eastern England. Later United States Admiral of the Fleet, William F. Halsey paid tribute to Australian Coastwatchers, "The Coastwatchers saved Guadalcanal, and Guadalcanal saved the South Pacific."

47. Morison, *Struggle for Guadalcanal*, p. 15; and Hough, *Pearl Harbor to Guadalcanal*, p. 298.

48. Smith, *Bloody Ridge*, p. 103; and Hough, *Pearl Harbor to Guadalcanal*, p. 298.

49. Zimmerman, *The Guadalcanal Campaign*, p. 78–79.

50. Frank, *Guadalcanal*, p. 197.

51. Smith, *Bloody Ridge*, p. 79, 91–92 & 94–95.

52. Griffith, *Battle for Guadalcanal*, p. 113; and Frank, *Guadalcanal*, pp. 198–199, 205, and 266.

53. Morison, *Struggle for Guadalcanal*, p. 113–114.

54. Frank, *Guadalcanal*, p. 201–203; Griffith, *Battle for Guadalcanal*, p. 116–124; and Smith, *Bloody Ridge*, p. 87–112.

55. Frank, *Guadalcanal*, p. 218–219.

56. Frank, *Guadalcanal*, p. 219–220; and Smith, *Bloody Ridge*, p. 113–115 & 243. Most of the men in Ichiki's second echelon were from Asahikawa, Hokkaidō. "Kuma" refers to the brown bears that lived in that area.

57. Frank, *Guadalcanal,* p. 220; and Smith, *Bloody Ridge,* p. 121.

58. Zimmerman, *Guadalcanal Campaign,* p. 80; and Griffith, *Battle for Guadalcanal,* p. 125.

59. Hough, *Pearl Harbor to Guadalcanal,* p. 298–299; Frank, *Guadalcanal,* p. 221–222; Smith, *Bloody Ridge,* p. 129; and Griffith, *Battle for Guadalcanal,* p. 129–130.

60. Griffith, *Battle for Guadalcanal,* p. 130–132; Frank, *Guadalcanal,* p. 221–222; and Smith, *Bloody Ridge,* p. 130.

61. Frank, *Guadalcanal,* p. 223 & 225–226; Griffith, *Battle for Guadalcanal,* p. 132 & 134–135; and Smith, *Bloody Ridge,* p. 130–131, 138.

62. Smith, *Bloody Ridge,* p. 161–167. The Marine defenders that finally defeated Kokusho's charge were most likely from the U.S. 11th Marine Regiment with assistance from the 1st Pioneer Battalion (Smith, p. 167; and Frank, p. 235).

63. Smith, *Bloody Ridge,* p. 162–193; Frank, *Guadalcanal,* p. 237–246; and Griffith, *Battle for Guadalcanal,* p. 141–147.

64. Griffith, *Battle for Guadalcanal,* p. 144; and Smith, *Bloody Ridge,* p. 184–194.

65. Smith, *Bloody Ridge,* p. 197–198.

66. Evans, *Japanese Navy,* p. 179–180; Frank, *Guadalcanal,* p. 247–252; Griffith, *Battle for Guadalcanal,* p. 156; and Smith, *Bloody Ridge,* p. 198–200.

67. Frank, *Guadalcanal,* p. 263.

68. Frank, *Guadalcanal*, p. 264–265.

69. Frank, *Guadalcanal*, p. 272.

70. Griffith, *Battle for Guadalcanal*, p. 152; Frank, *Guadalcanal*, p. 224, 251–254, & 266; Jersey, *Hell's Islands*, p. 248–249; and Smith, *Bloody Ridge*, p. 132 & 158.

71. Smith, *Bloody Ridge*, p. 204; and Frank, *Guadalcanal*, p. 270.

72. Smith, *Bloody Ridge*, p. 204–215, Frank, *Guadalcanal*, p. 269–274, Zimmerman, *The Guadalcanal Campaign*, p. 96–101.

73. Griffith, *Battle for Guadalcanal*, p. 169–176; Frank, *Guadalcanal*, p. 282–290; and Hough, *Pearl Harbor to Guadalcanal*, p. 318–322.

74. Frank, *Guadalcanal*, p. 290–291. Fifteen of the Marines and the three U.S. Navy sailors were killed when their Higgins boat carrying them from Tulagi to Aola Bay on Guadalcanal was lost. One of the Japanese killed in the raid was "Ishimoto," a Japanese intelligence agent who had worked in the Solomon Islands area prior to the war and had murdered two Catholic priests and two nuns at Tasimboko on September 3, 1942.

75. Rottman, *Japanese Army*, p. 61; Griffith, *Battle for Guadalcanal*, p. 152; Frank, *Guadalcanal*, p. 224, 251–254, 266–268, & 289–290; Dull, *Imperial Japanese Navy*, p. 225–226; and Smith, *Bloody Ridge*, p. 132 & 158.

76. Frank, *Guadalcanal*, p. 293–297; Cook, *Cape Esperance*, p. 16, 19–20; Morison, *Struggle for Guadalcanal*, p. 147–149; and Dull, *Imperial Japanese Navy*, p. 225. Since not all

of the Task Force 64 warships were available, Scott's force was designated as Task Group 64.2. The U.S. destroyers were from Squadron 12, commanded by Captain Robert G. Tobin in *Farenholt*.

77. Frank, *Guadalcanal*, p. 295–296; Hackett, *HIJMS Aoba: Tabular Record of Movement*; Cook, *Cape Esperance*, p. 31 and 57; Morison, *Struggle for Guadalcanal*, p. 149–151; D'Albas, *Death of a Navy*, p. 183; and Dull, *Imperial Japanese Navy*, p. 226.

78. Frank, *Guadalcanal*, p. 299–324; Morison, *Struggle for Guadalcanal*, p. 154–171; and Dull, *Imperial Japanese Navy*, p. 226–230.

79. Frank, *Guadalcanal*, p. 313–315. The 16th was from the 2nd Division and the 230th from the 38th Division.

80. Evans, *Japanese Navy*, p. 181–182; Frank, *Guadalcanal*, p. 315–320; Morison, *Struggle for Guadalcanal*, p. 171–175. Raizo Tanaka commanded Destroyer Squadron 2 which was part of the battleship's screen.

81. Frank, *Guadalcanal*, p. 319–321.

82. "Martello: An Unsung Hero", Published Oral History.

83. Frank, *Guadalcanal*, p. 321–326; Hough, *Pearl Harbor to Guadalcanal*, p. 327–328.

84. Shaw, *First Offensive*, p. 34; and Rottman, *Japanese Army*, p. 63.

85. Rottman, *Japanese Army*, p. 61; Frank, *Guadalcanal*, p. 289–340; Hough, *Pearl Harbor to Guadalcanal*, p. 322–330; Griffith, *Battle for Guadalcanal*, p. 186–187; Dull,

Imperial Japanese Navy, p. 226–230; Morison, *Struggle for Guadalcanal*, p. 149–171. The Japanese troops delivered to Guadalcanal during this time comprised the entire 2nd (Sendai) Infantry Division, two battalions from the 38th Infantry Division, and various artillery, tank, engineer, and other support units. Kawaguchi's forces also included what remained of the 3rd Battalion, 124th Infantry Regiment which was originally part of the 35th Infantry Brigade commanded by Kawaguchi during the Battle of Edson's Ridge.

86. Miller, *Guadalcanal: The First Offensive*, p. 155; Frank, *Guadalcanal*, p. 339–341; Hough, *Pearl Harbor to Guadalcanal*, p. 330; Rottman, *Japanese Army*, p. 62; Griffith, *Battle for Guadalcanal*, p. 187–188. Hyakutake sent a member of his staff, Colonel Masanobu Tsuji to monitor the 2nd Division's progress along the trail and to report to him on whether the attack could begin on October 22 as scheduled. Masanobu Tsuji has been identified by some historians as the most likely culprit behind the Bataan death march.

87. Griffith, *Battle for Guadalcanal*, p. 193; Frank, *Guadalcanal*, p. 346–348; Rottman, *Japanese Army*, p. 62.

88. Hough, *Pearl Harbor to Guadalcanal*, p. 332–333; Frank, *Guadalcanal*, p. 349–350; Rottman, *Japanese Army*, p. 62–63; Griffith, *Battle for Guadalcanal*, p. 195–196; Miller, *Guadalcanal: The First Offensive*, p. 157–158. The Marines lost 2 killed in the action. Japanese infantry losses aren't recorded but were, according to Frank, "unquestionably severe." Griffith says that 600 Japanese soldiers were killed.

Only 17 of the 44 members of the 1st Independent Tank Company survived the battle.

89. Frank, *Guadalcanal*, p. 361–362.

90. Hough, *Pearl Harbor to Guadalcanal*, p. 336; Frank, *Guadalcanal*, p. 353–362; Griffith, *Battle for Guadalcanal*, p. 197–204; Miller, *Guadalcanal: The First Offensive*, p. 160–162; Miller, *Cactus Air Force*, p. 147–151; Lundstrom, *Guadalcanal Campaign*, p. 343–352. The 164th became the first Army unit to engage in combat in the war and was later awarded the Presidential Unit Citation.

91. Frank, *Guadalcanal*, 363–406, 418, 424, and 553; Zimmerman, *Guadalcanal Campaign*, p. 122–123; Griffith, *Battle for Guadalcanal*, p. 204; Hough, *Pearl Harbor to Guadalcanal*, p. 337; Rottman, *Japanese Army*, p. 63. Silver Stars awarded to Sgt. Norman Greber of Ohio, Pvt. Don Reno of Texas, Pvt. Jack Bando of Oregon, Pvt. Stan Ralph of New York, and Cpl. Michael Randall of New York.

92. Morison, *Struggle for Guadalcanal*, p. 199–207; Frank, *Guadalcanal*, p. 368–378; Dull, *Imperial Japanese Navy*, p. 235–237. Admiral Chester Nimitz, Allied Commander in Chief of Pacific Forces, replaced Ghormley with Halsey on October 18.

93. Dull, *Imperial Japanese Navy*, p. 237–244; Frank, *Guadalcanal*, p. 379–r03; Morison, *Struggle for Guadalcanal*, p. 207–224.

94. Hough, *Pearl Harbor to Guadalcanal*, p. 343; Hammel, *Guadalcanal*, p. 135; Griffith, *Battle for Guadalcanal*, p. 214–15; Frank, *Guadalcanal*, p. 411; Anderson, *Guadalcanal*;

Shaw, *First Offensive*, p. 40–41; Zimmerman, *Guadalcanal Campaign*, p. 130–31.

95. Shaw, *First Offensive*, p. 40–41; Griffith, *Battle for Guadalcanal*, p. 215–218; Hough, *Pearl Harbor to Guadalcanal*, p. 344–345; Zimmerman, *Guadalcanal Campaign*, p. 131–133; Frank, *Guadalcanal*, p. 412–420; Hammel, *Guadalcanal*, p. 138–139.

96. Zimmerman, *Guadalcanal Campaign*, p. 133–138; Griffith, *Battle for Guadalcanal*, p. 217–219; Hough, *Pearl Harbor to Guadalcanal*, p. 347–348; Frank, *Guadalcanal*, p. 414–418; Miller, *Guadalcanal*, p. 195–197; Hammel, *Guadalcanal*, p. 141; Shaw, *First Offensive*, p. 41–42; Jersey, *Hell's Islands*, p. 297. Jersey states that the troops landed were from the 2nd Company, 230th Infantry commanded by 1st Lt Tamotsu Shinno plus the 6th Battery, 28th Mountain Artillery Regiment with the two guns.

97. Zimmerman, *Guadalcanal Campaign*, p. 133–141; Griffith, *Battle for Guadalcanal*, p. 217–223; Hough, *Pearl Harbor to Guadalcanal*, p. 347–350; Frank, *Guadalcanal*, p. 414–423; Miller, *Guadalcanal*, p. 195–200; Hammel, *Guadalcanal*, p. 141–144; Shaw, *First Offensive*, p. 41–42; Jersey, *Hell's Islands*, p. 297–305.

98. Peatross, *Bless 'em All*, p. 132–133; Frank, *Guadalcanal*, p. 420–421; Hoffman, *Long Patrol*. The two 2nd Raider companies sent to Aola were Companies C and E.

99. Hough, *Pearl Harbor to Guadalcanal*, p. 348–350; Shaw, *First Offensive*, p. 42–43; Frank, *Guadalcanal*, p. 420–424; Griffith, *Battle for Guadalcanal*, p. 246; Miller, *Guadalcanal*,

p. 197–200; Zimmerman, *Guadalcanal Campaign*, p. 136–145.

100. Frank, *Guadalcanal*, p. 420–421, 424–25, 493–497; Anderson, *Guadalcanal*; Hough, *Pearl Harbor to Guadalcanal*, p. 350–58; Zimmerman, *Guadalcanal Campaign*, p. 150–52.

101. Hammel, *Guadalcanal: Decision at Sea*, 41–46.

102. Hammel, *Guadalcanal: Decision at Sea*, 93.

103. Hammel, *Guadalcanal: Decision at Sea*, 37.

104. Hammel, *Guadalcanal: Decision at Sea*, 38–39; Frank, *Guadalcanal*, p. 429–430. The American reinforcements totaled 5,500 men and included the 1st Marine Aviation Engineer Battalion, replacements for ground and air units, the 4th Marine Replacement Battalion, two battalions of the US Army's 182nd Infantry Regiment, and ammunition and supplies.

105. Frank, *Guadalcanal*, 432; Hammel, *Guadalcanal: Decision at Sea*, 50–90.

106. Hara, *Japanese Destroyer Captain*, 137.

107. Hammel, *Guadalcanal: Decision at Sea*, p. 92.

108. Hammel, *Guadalcanal: Decision at Sea*, 99–107.

109. New moon Nov 8, 1942 15:19 hours. http://eclipse.gsfc.nasa.gov/phase/phases1901.html

110. Frank, *Guadalcanal*, p. 428–461; Hammel, *Guadalcanal: Decision at Sea*, p. 103–401; Hara, *Japanese Destroyer Captain*, p. 137–156.

111. Frank, *Guadalcanal,* p. 465–474; Hammel, *Guadalcanal: Decision at Sea,* p. 298–345.

112. Hammel, *Guadalcanal: Decision at Sea,* 349–395; Frank, *Guadalcanal,* p. 469–486.

113. Frank, *Guadalcanal,* p. 484–488, 527; Hammel, *Guadalcanal: Decision at Sea,* p. 391–395.

114. Dull, p. 261, Frank, p. 497–499.

115. Evans, p. 197–198, Crenshaw, p. 136, Frank, p. 499–502.

116. Hara, p. 160–161, Roscoe, p. 206, Dull, p. 262, Evans, p. 197–198, Crenshaw, p. 137, Toland, p. 419, Frank, p. 502, Morison, p. 295.

117. Dull, p. 262–263, Evans, p. 198–199, Crenshaw, p. 137, Morison, p. 297, Frank, p. 502–504.

118. Brown, p. 124–125, USSBS, p. 139, Roscoe, p. 206, Dull,p. 262, Crenshaw, p. 26–33, Kilpatrick, p. 139–142, Morison, p. 294–296, Frank, p. 504.

119. Hara, p. 161–164, Dull, p. 265, Evans, p. 199–202, Crenshaw, p. 34, 63, 139–151, Morison, p. 297–305, Frank, p. 507–510.

120. Dull, p. 265, Crenshaw, p. 56–66, Morison, p. 303–312, Frank, p. 510–515.

121. Frank, *Guadalcanal,* p. 527.

122. Dull, p. 266–267; Evans, p. 203–205; Morison, p. 318–319; Frank, p. 518–521.

123. Dull, *Imperial Japanese Navy,* p. 261.

124. Frank, *Guadalcanal*, pp. 428–92; Dull, *Imperial Japanese Navy*, pp. 245–69.

125. Bergerund, *Fire in the Sky*.

126. Weinberg (1995), pp. 208–209.

127. Weinburg (1995), pp. 209–210.

Books

Bergerud, Eric M. (1997). Touched with Fire: The Land War in the South Pacific. Penguin. ISBN 0-14-024696-7.

Dull, Paul S. (1978). A Battle History of the Imperial Japanese Navy, 1941-1945. Naval Institute Press. ISBN 0-87021-097-1.

Evans, David C. (1986 (2nd Edition)). "The Struggle for Guadalcanal", The Japanese Navy in World War II: In the Words of Former Japanese Naval Officers. Annapolis, Maryland: Naval Institute Press. ISBN 0-87021-316-4.

Frank, Richard (1990). Guadalcanal: The Definitive Account of the Landmark Battle. New York: Random House. ISBN 0-394-58875-4.

Griffith, Samuel B. (1963). The Battle for Guadalcanal. Champaign, Illinois, USA: University of Illinois Press. ISBN 0-252-06891-2.

Hammel, Eric (1999). Carrier Clash: The Invasion of Guadalcanal & The Battle of the Eastern Solomons August 1942. St. Paul, MN, USA: Zenith Press. 0760320527.

Hammel, Eric (1999). Carrier Strike: The Battle of the Santa Cruz Islands, October 1942. Pacifica Press. ISBN 0-935553-37-1.

Jersey, Stanley Coleman (2008). Hell's Islands: The Untold Story of Guadalcanal. College Station, Texas: Texas A&M University Press. ISBN 1-58544-616-5.

Kilpatrick, C. W. (1987). Naval Night Battles of the Solomons. Exposition Press. ISBN 0-682-40333-4.

Loxton, Bruce; Chris Coulthard-Clark (1997). The Shame of Savo: Anatomy of a Naval Disaster. Australia: Allen & Unwin Pty Ltd. ISBN 1-86448-286-9.

Lundstrom, John B. (2005 (New edition)). First Team And the Guadalcanal Campaign: Naval Fighter Combat from August to November 1942. Naval Institute Press. ISBN 1-59114-472-8.

McGee, William L. (2002). The Solomons Campaigns, 1942-1943: From Guadalcanal to Bougainville—Pacific War Turning Point, Volume 2 (Amphibious Operations in the South Pacific in WWII). BMC Publications. ISBN 0-9701678-7-3.

Miller, Thomas G. (1969). Cactus Air Force. Admiral Nimitz Foundation. ISBN 0-934841-17-9.

Morison, Samuel Eliot (1958). The Struggle for Guadalcanal, August 1942 – February 1943, vol. 5 of History of United

States Naval Operations in World War II. Boston: Little, Brown and Company. ISBN 0-316-58305-7.

Murray, Williamson; Allan R. Millett (2001). A War To Be Won: Fighting the Second World War. United States of America: Belknap Press. ISBN 0-674-00680-1.

Peatross, Oscar F.; John P. McCarthy and John Clayborne (editors) (1995). Bless 'em All: The Raider Marines of World War II. Review. ISBN 0965232506.

Rottman, Gordon L.; Dr. Duncan Anderson (consultant editor) (2005). Japanese Army in World War II: The South Pacific and New Guinea, 1942-43. Oxford and New York: Osprey. ISBN 1-84176-870-7.

Smith, Michael T. (2000). Bloody Ridge: The Battle That Saved Guadalcanal. New York: Pocket. ISBN 0-7434-6321-8.

Weinberg, Gerhard L. (1995). Germany, Hitler and World War II. Cambridge University Press. ISBN 0-5215-6626-6.

Web

Anderson, Charles R. (1993). GUADALCANAL (brochure). U.S. GOVERNMENT PRINTING OFFICE. Retrieved on 2006-07-09.

Cagney, James (2007). The Battle for Guadalcanal (javascript). HistoryAnimated.com. Retrieved on 2006-05-17.- Interactive animation of the battle

Chen, C. Peter (2004 - 2006). Guadalcanal Campaign. World War II Database. Retrieved on 2006-05-17.

Craven, Wesley Frank; James Lea Cate. Vol. IV, The Pacific: Guadalcanal to Saipan, August 1942 to July 1944. The Army Air Forces in World War II. U.S. Office of Air Force History. Retrieved on October 20, 2006.

de Vos, M.E. (2003 - 2006). Map of Guadalcanal.

Donahue, Jr.,, Jim (2005). Guadalcanal Journal. Retrieved on 2006-11-08.

Flahavin, Peter (2004). Guadalcanal Battle Sites, 1942-2004. Retrieved on 2006-08-02.- Web site with many pictures of Guadalcanal battle sites from 1942 and how they look now.

Garrett, Rube (2003). A Marine Diary: My Experiences on Guadalcanal.

Gillespie, Oliver A. (1952). The Official History of New Zealand in the Second World War, 1939–1945; The Battle for the Solomons (Chapter 7). New Zealand Electronic Text Center. Retrieved on July 11, 2006.

Hoffman, Jon T. (1995). FROM MAKIN TO BOUGAINVILLE: Marine Raiders in the Pacific War (brochure). WORLD WAR II COMMEMORATIVE SERIES. Marine Corps Historical Center. Retrieved on 2006-08-29.

Hoffman, Jon T.. SILK CHUTES AND HARD FIGHTING: US. Marine Corps Parachute Units in World War II (English). Commemorative series 1. Marine Corps History and Museums Division. Retrieved on December 26, 2006.

Hough, Frank O.; Ludwig, Verle E., and Shaw, Henry I., Jr.. Pearl Harbor to Guadalcanal. History of U.S. Marine Corps Operations in World War II. Retrieved on 2006-05-16.

Inui, Genjirou. My Guadalcanal. Retrieved on 2007-01-16.- First-hand account of the campaign by an officer in the Japanese 28th Infantry Regiment.

Mersky, Peter B. (1993). Time of the Aces: Marine Pilots in the Solomons, 1942-1944 (English). Marines in World

War II Commemorative Series. History and Museums Division, Headquarters, U.S. Marine Corps. Retrieved on October 20, 2006.

Miller, John Jr. (1949). GUADALCANAL: THE FIRST OFFENSIVE. UNITED STATES ARMY IN WORLD WAR II. Retrieved on 2006-07-04.

Hirose (full name not available) (2007). Report of a Japanese soldier about the battle of Guadalcanal (English and German). Retrieved on February 16, 2007.

Shaw, Henry I. (1992). First Offensive: The Marine Campaign For Guadalcanal. Marines in World War II Commemorative Series. Retrieved on 2006-07-25.

U.S. Army Center of Military History. Japanese Operations in the Southwest Pacific Area, Volume II - Part I. Reports of General MacArthur. Retrieved on 2006-12-08.- Translation of the official record by the Japanese Demobilization Bureaux detailing the Imperial Japanese Army and Navy's participation in the Southwest Pacific area of the Pacific War.

Zimmerman, John L. (1949). The Guadalcanal Campaign. Marines in World War II Historical Monograph. Retrieved on 2006-07-04.

Further reading

Alexander, Joseph H. (2000). Edson's Raiders: The 1st Marine Raider Battalion in World War II. Naval Institute Press. ISBN 1-55750-020-7.

Christ, James F. (2007). Battalion of the Damned: The 1st Marine Paratroopers at Gavutu and Bloody Ridge, 1942. Naval Institute Press. ISBN 1591141141.

Clemens, Martin (2004 (reissue)). Alone on Guadalcanal: A Coastwatcher's Story. Bluejacket Books. ISBN 1-59114-124-9.

Coggins, Jack (1972). The campaign for Guadalcanal;: A battle that made history. DoubleDay. ISBN 0385043546.

D'Albas, Andrieu (1965). Death of a Navy: Japanese Naval Action in World War II. Devin-Adair Pub. ISBN 0-8159-5302-X.

Feldt, Eric Augustus (1946 (original text), 1991 (this edition)). The Coastwatchers. Victoria, Australia: Penguin Books. ISBN 0140149260.

Leckie, Robert (2001 (reissue)). Helmet for my Pillow. ibooks, Inc.. ISBN 1-59687-092-3.

Hara, Tameichi (1961). Japanese Destroyer Captain. New York & Toronto: Ballantine Books. ISBN 0-345-27894-1.

Hersey, John (2002 (Paperback edition)). Into the Valley: Marines at Guadalcanal. Bison Books. ISBN 0803273282.

Hoyt, Edwin P. (1982). Guadalcanal. Military Heritage Press. ISBN 0880291842.

Hubler, Richard G.; Dechant, John A (1944). Flying Leathernecks - The Complete Record of Marine Corps Aviation in Action 1941–1944.. Garden City, New York: Doubleday, Doran & Co., Inc.

Lord, Walter (1977 (Reissue 2006)). Lonely Vigil; Coastwatchers of the Solomons. New York: Naval Institute Press. ISBN 1-59114-466-3.

Lundstrom, John B. (2006). Black Shoe Carrier Admiral: Frank Jack Fletcher at Coral Seas, Midway & Guadalcanal. Annapolis, Maryland, USA: Naval Institute Press. ISBN 1-59114-475-2.

Parkin, Robert Sinclair (1995). Blood on the Sea: American Destroyers Lost in World War II. Da Capo Press. ISBN 0-306-81069-7.

Poor, Henry Varnum; Henry A. Mustin & Colin G. Jameson (1994). The Battles of Cape Esperance, 11 October 1942 and Santa Cruz Islands, 26 October 1942 (Combat Narratives. Solomon Islands Campaign, 4–5). Naval Historical Center. ISBN 0-945274-21-1.

Rose, Lisle Abbott (2002). The Ship that Held the Line: The USS Hornet and the First Year of the Pacific War. Bluejacket Books. ISBN 1-55750-008-8.

Rottman, Gordon L.; Dr. Duncan Anderson (consultant editor) (2004). US Marine Corps Pacific Theatre of Operations 1941–43. Oxford: Osprey. ISBN 1-84176-518-X.

Stafford, Edward P.; Paul Stillwell (Introduction) (2002 (reissue)). The Big E: The Story of the USS Enterprise. Naval Institute Press. ISBN 1-55750-998-0.

Tregaskis, Richard (1943). Guadalcanal Diary. Random House. ISBN 0-679-64023-1.

Twining, Merrill B. (1996). No Bended Knee: The Battle for Guadalcanal. Novato, CA, USA: Presidio Press. ISBN 0-89141-826-1.

Audio/visual

Adams, M. Clay (Director). (1952) Victory at Sea- Episode 6: Guadalcanal [Video documentary]. National Broadcasting Company (NBC) Film. — One episode from a 26-episode series about naval combat during World War II.

Malick, Terrence (Director). (1998) The Thin Red Line [Feature-length film]. 20th Century Fox Home Entertainment. — Film adaptation of James Jones' fictional, dramatic novel of the same title set on Guadalcanal.

Marton, Andrew (Director). (1964) The Thin Red Line [Feature-length film]. Allied Artists Pictures. — Film adaptation of James Jones' fictional, dramatic novel of the same title set on Guadalcanal.

Montgomery, Robert (Director). (1960) The Gallant Hours [Feature-length film]. United Artists. — Biopic about Admiral Halsey during the Guadalcanal campaign

Ray, Nicholas (Director). (1951) Flying Leathernecks [Feature-length film]. RKO Radio Pictures. - Fictional drama about U.S. Marine pilots involved in the Battle of Guadalcanal.

Seiler, Lewis (Director). (1943) Guadalcanal Diary [Feature-length film]. 20th Century Fox Film Corporation. - Film adaptation of Tregaskis' book referenced in "Books" section above.

www.ingramcontent.com/pod-product-compliance
Lightning Source LLC
Chambersburg PA
CBHW022020090426
42739CB00006BA/214